TALES OF THE
REDUNDANCE KID
or THE BEDSIDE
BARRY NORMAN

TALES OF THE
REDUNDANCE KID

or THE BEDSIDE
BARRY NORMAN

Preface by NICHOLAS MONSARRAT

Drawings by John Kent

VNR VAN NOSTRAND REINHOLD

First published 1975 by
Van Nostrand Reinhold Company Limited
Molly Millars Lane, Wokingham
Berkshire, England

ISBN 0 442 30152 9

Printed by Jolly & Barber Limited
Rugby, Warwickshire, England

———————————————————————

Other Van Nostrand Reinhold offices:

450 West 33rd Street
New York, NY 10001

1410 Birchmount Road
Scarborough M1P 2E7, Ontario

17 Queen Street
Mitcham, Victoria 3132, Melbourne

Contents

AUTHOR'S NOTE

Except where otherwise stated all the pieces in this book were originally printed in *The Guardian* and what I say is, God bless *The Guardian*.

Preface

Naturally, I do not read *The Guardian*, having been strictly brought up – and brought up also in Liverpool, where this newspaper's former title, the *Manchester Guardian*, ensured that it was impounded at the frontier. Barry Norman writes leaders for *The Guardian*.

I do not read *The Times*, since its recent label, "Top paper for Top people", disqualifies me. Barry Norman does show-business interviews for *The Times*.

I have not read *The Observer* since 1936, when its otherwise gifted editor, J. L. Garvin, took it into the pro-Mussolini fascist camp. Barry Norman writes sports interviews for *The Observer*.

I *do* read the world's funniest strip cartoon, *Flook*, in the *Daily Mail*. But Barry Norman stopped doing funnies for *Flook* about a year ago.

I cannot watch BBC 1, since I live in Malta and have not paid enough for my TV set; nor listen to Radio 4's "Today" programme, for a similar reason. Barry Norman works for one of these as a film critic and the other as a "presenter".

But I know from my files (I keep files for sentimental reasons, like many a manicurist now married and going straight) that Barry Norman has interviewed me twice in the course of duty. On neither occasion did he make me sound more of a fool or a phoney than was necessary for the purposes of a newspaper coining its principal money out of what Sheridan called "the sneer insidious".

For that reason alone, I must ignore all these disqualifications, and give myself the pleasure of introducing *The Redundance Kid*.

Why its amusing and talented author was ever declared redundant, by any newspaper, really passes belief – until you stroll down Fleet Street and observe the chaps that weren't. But it happened to Barry Norman, and thus he diversified – if that has not become a dirty word, in a decade when Amalgamated Bone Manure can suddenly switch to Hot-Tip After-Shave Lotion ("Drives Women Mad – Smells like Money!"). He diversified to excellent purpose, as this book will show you.

He has a cunning gift for words which I envy – well, let's not fool around: he has a cunning gift for words. He is also very funny, and perceptive, and adroit – and above all fair: not for him the grubbed-up fact which becomes the snide fancy. (You fool! That's why he was redundant!)

He even writes novels, although, as a competing novelist in a shrinking market, I would be nuts to recommend any of them. Let's begin and end with *The Redundance Kid*, which–and now I must dig as deep and as wide as any trendy grave-robber for the quotable phrase which might get my own name into the ads – which, like a long-ago black-and-white five-pound note, is worth infinitely more than the paper it is printed on.

I think I have successfully fudged that one. The Honest Fiver went out with Chastity, and neither got back. But you, suspicious ferret that you are, have guessed right on one point. Barry Norman, and his film-producer father before him, Leslie Norman, were and are friends of mine. God grant me more of the same good quality.

NICHOLAS MONSARRAT

Introduction

I was made redundant by the *Daily Mail* at about half-past nine on the night of Friday, March 12, 1971 and I mention this now not from any desire to brag but as a matter of historical fact. I should also like to take this opportunity to thank those responsible, whoever they may have been, for what at the time seemed an unkind – to say nothing of crass and insensitive – act; because, from a professional point of view, making me redundant turned out to be quite the nicest thing the *Daily Mail* did for me in all the thirteen years I worked for it.

I'm not, mark you, suggesting that as experiences go it was a particularly pleasant one and, as to that, my reactions to redundancy – both immediate and after the passage of a few weeks – will also be found in this Introduction and much as I jotted them down at the time. The point is, however, that faced with redundancy what does one do? Well, to start with I regarded myself as a redundant show-business editor, the post I had held on the *Mail* until all the unpleasantness occurred, and my initial aim was to make myself, as rapidly as possible, an employed show business editor. Unfortunately, in the whole of Fleet Street there existed only three or four of the breed and my colleagues who filled the position on other papers showed a deplorably selfish reluctance to move over and make way for me.

So, as the rest of March and April went by and the clamour for my services as a staffman on other national newspapers – if it existed at all – was so high-pitched as to be undiscernible to the human ear, I began to realise that what I had become, unpalatable though it might be to one who had been accustomed to hobnobbing with the likes of Lord Olivier and getting smashed out of his mind in the company of Richard Burton, was an out-of-work freelance journalist.

Well, there are worse things to be. It's much easier, after all, to scrape a living as a freelance journalist than, say, as a freelance company chairman. You're much likelier to get a positive response if you approach the London *Evening Standard* and say, "Can I do a spot of freelance writing for you?" than if you walked into the head office of I.C.I. offering to do a bit of freelance managing-directing. All a freelance journalist needs in order to ply his trade is a typewriter, a supply of paper, a telephone and a few ideas.

So a freelance journalist is what I became. I had one initial stroke of good fortune. On the Monday after I was redunded, John

Higgins, the assistant editor of *The Times*, took me to lunch and asked if I would do one television review a week for him at a fee of £15 a time. Now even allowing for the fact that a gross income of £15 a week was hardly likely to keep me, my wife, my two children, one dog, two guinea pigs and a mortgage in the manner to which we'd become accustomed, this was very nice of him, because even a once-weekly gig as a telly critic on *The Times* is an excellent shop window. In fact there's only one better in the whole of Fleet Street and that's *The Guardian*, of which more later. This piece of luck (for which I shall be ever grateful), this base from which to begin operations was immensely helpful as I began the distasteful business of hustling my wares around the street of misadventure. Strange editors, who would otherwise regard one with deep suspicion as though redundancy were an anti-social and infectious disease – which I suppose is what it is – would look incredibly relieved when I mentioned my connection, tenuous though it might be, with *The Times*, no doubt feeling that I had come through the incubation period and was unlikely to strike them with the illness that I had suffered.

Beyond that, however, I did something which, I think, was rather clever. Experience had taught me that it's only when you look as if you're prosperous that people want to employ you. Go about looking relaxed and well-to-do and they clamour for your services. Turn up, on the other hand, down-at-heel and clearly in need of work and money and you can't even get arrested. Therefore I invested a little of my redundancy payoff in some new shirts, suits and ties and appeared everywhere in public in the very best clothes I had. I also did my social drinking not in low pubs but in expensive wine bars much frequented by the kind of people I hoped would employ me. Maybe that sounds kind of creepy; maybe it was. But when you're redundant, you don't care too much. You don't want favours: all you want is a chance to prove that you can do the job, that in fact you're not really redundant at all because you still have much to offer. And if the way to get that opportunity is to exercise a mild confidence trick then, you argue, why not? Anyway, it seemed to work, although in retrospect I can see it's possible that my sartorial elegance and pretence of affluence did more to boost my own self-esteem than to impress other people. In any event I became busy – not prosperous but busy. I wrote TV reviews for *The Times*, theatre reviews for *Plays and Players*, feature articles for the Central Office of Information, gossip paragraphs for *The Sunday Mirror*, interviews for *The Observer* colour supplement. For some while, though, I was still prickly and over-sensitive, looking for slights and insults where none was intended. If anybody rebuffed, or even appeared to rebuff, me I swore that some day I would exact a terrible revenge – and I'd still do it now if I could only remember their names.

In midsummer I had another slice of luck. Thanks to the Fairy Godfather activities of my friend Bernard Levin (than whom no kinder man ever trod the face of the earth and who, unsolicited by me, had written to several newspaper editors suggesting that if they were to recruit any of the discarded Mailmen I might be worthy of their attention, since I was unlikely to get drunk and offer violence to the proprietor or indecent propositions to his wife) I found myself acting as a sort of jobbing leader writer to *The Guardian*. The idea was that I should go in a couple of times a week while the regular leader writers took turns to have a holiday and write amusing editorials, possibly because I clearly wasn't fit to write serious ones. Well, this very pleasant job went on for about three or four months until one day *The Guardian* was so overrun with leader writers that the editor's secretary had to vacate her desk and pace up and down the general office for an hour or two while I used her typewriter to bash out my piece.

At the end of that day the editor, Alastair Hetherington, said with what I took to be genuine regret that he really couldn't justify having me on his leader-writing strength any more. So I said, feeling I had nothing to lose: "Why don't I write a weekly column for you instead?" And he said: "That's not a bad idea but you'll have to see if Peter Preston, the features editor, agrees." On almost any other paper in Fleet Street if the editor thought it would be a good idea for me to write a column then there would be no further discussion of the matter. But one of the splendid things about *The Guardian* is that the heads of department have a high degree of autonomy. So if Peter Preston didn't fancy me as a columnist there would be no way I could become one.

I went in search of Peter at once and, fortunately, found him in the lavatory. So I took up my position in the next stall and broached the subject of my writing a column while we both stared thought-fully at the wall. And when I'd finished my sales pitch, he said– and in retrospect I suppose he could hardly have said anything else, considering the circumstances in which I'd trapped him: "That seems quite a reasonable idea. Can you start next week?" And I said yes, I certainly could and we, as it were, shook on it.

Well, round about the same time I had a phone call from another great friend, Wally Fawkes, who is not only a sublime jazz musician but is also, of course, widely known as Trog, the cartoonist. "Let's have lunch," he said.

"Great," I said. "It's time we had a few drinks and a chat."

"No, no," said Wally, gravely. "I approach you as a business man. This is a time for grown-ups' talk. See you in El Vino's."

So we met in El Vino's and he bought a bottle of champagne and Keith McKenzie, the arts director of the *Daily Mail*, bought a bottle of champagne and then we all went to have lunch in an Italian restaurant across the road and I bought a litre of wine and at some stage during the slurred and inarticulate conversation that followed it was agreed that I should write the script for *Flook* in, of all papers, the *Mail* – Wally being the creator of that excellent strip cartoon.

Thus at the end of that year I was collaborating with Wally on *Flook* and I was also, I believe, the first person ever to write regularly every week for both *The Guardian* and *The Times* under his own name, a record of which I am insufferably proud. Also at the end of that year I had another encounter in a public lavatory. Well, some years are like that. Some years you don't meet anybody in public lavatories; other years every time you have a leak it's like attending a soirée. Anyway, I was looking to my own business in the loo at the Dorchester after some official lunch and Martin Jackson, then of the *Daily Express* and a sort of commissar in the TV section of the Critics' Circle installed himself alongside me.

"We're looking for someone," he said, "to go on *Late Night Line-Up* and talk about the critics' nomination for TV Play of the Year. Do you fancy it?"

"How much?" I said.

"Oh, I dunno," he said. "About twenty quid, I suppose."

"I fancy it," I said. We left the stalls and moved across to the hand basins.

"Oh, by the way, Martin," I said, "what is this play I'm talking about?"

So about a dozen of us appeared on BBC 2 to discuss the television awards of the year – a pretty spurious event, I'm bound to say, since we television critics had nothing to give the award winners except our good wishes. And a few days later I had a phone call from a man named Iain Johnstone, of whom (and this shows what sort of a critic I was) I'd never heard and he said: "I produce a programme called *Film 72* on BBC 1. Would you like to come and present it for me?" And I said I'd be glad to but honesty compelled me to point out that I'd never done anything remotely like that in my life.

"Oh, that's all right," he said. "It's easy." And such is this great man's grasp of psychology that I'd actually been doing the programme for six weeks before I realised it wasn't easy at all. The remarkable thing about both television and radio is that they take people from entirely different walks of life and hurl them straight into the deep end, gathering round with mild curiosity to see whether they bob up to the surface or go down like a rock. There's no training period. My advance preparation for presenting *Film 72* consisted of half a bottle of Beaujolais, poured down my throat by Iain Johnstone, and took five-minute camera tests, the first to decide whether I looked too hideous for public consumption, the second to discover whether I could read an autocue without swivelling my eyes from side to side. It's the same with radio. When, in

September 1974, Alistair Osborne asked me if I'd like to join the *Today* programme on Radio 4 as one of the presenters I spent one Tuesday morning watching John Timpson and James Burke present it and then– it being now confidently assumed that I had a total grasp of the subject – I was asked to present it all by myself the following Saturday.

However, at this point you may well wonder why I've gone on about all this at such inordinate, and very possibly boring, length. Well, first of all it's an oblique and roundabout way of explaining how this present volume of bits and pieces came into being. But a more important point is that none of this could have happened if I hadn't been made redundant. Now I'm not suggesting redundancy is good for you (although, thank God, it's turned out to be very good for me so far); nor do I suggest that the reminiscences of a redundant journalist can be of much value to or provide a great deal of inspiration for a redundant car worker or research chemist. But redundancy is, after all, an occupational hazard of our times, no matter what your occupation may be, and there are perhaps a couple of general observations about it that I may be permitted to make. The first is that you have to be prepared to swallow a great unchewed lump of pride and start again several notches down the ladder from the point you'd reached when they opened the doors and chucked you out into the street. And the second is that the healthier reaction to redundancy is anger, not despair. If instead of saying, "How could they?", you can say, "Sod 'em", you are at least in the right frame of mind to fight back.

In the first year of hustling and knocking on strange doors as I tried to re-establish myself I took a lot of jobs which, a few months earlier, I would have scorned for fees which I would have regarded as an insult. And what caused me to do that and to work harder than I'd ever worked in my life was anger– a furious desire to prove to the *Daily Mail* and those responsible for uprooting me after so many years from my comfortable niche that they had made a mistake. And indeed there came a time when I felt I'd done it; I'd shown them all. But, of course, by then it didn't matter any more. Life had moved on. I was better off without the *Daily Mail* and no doubt the *Mail* was a great deal better off without me. A nice arrangement as it turned out but I'll tell you something – I shouldn't like to have to go through it all again.

The foregoing was written earlier this year, by way of establishing my credentials such as they are. The first part of what follows now was written two days after I received my redundancy notice – on the morning of Sunday, March 14, 1971 to be absolutely precise. I jotted it down purely for my own records and at the instigation of my friend Bernard Levin who, in his wisdom, said that if I didn't write it immediately and while it was fresh in my mind I would certainly forget it and he was right. On reading it through before including it in this book I thought at first of re-writing it, polishing it up, adding a few jokes and then I thought, no, what the hell. If it has any interest at all at this stage it can only be because it reflects exactly what I felt at the time. In retrospect I can see that some of it turned out to be wrong. In fact, both the Daily Mail *and the* Daily Sketch *died in that merger and a new paper, better than either of the old ones, gradually took shape under the borrowed banner of the* Daily Mail.

The news came through early in the evening while I was having a drink with a friend in the Mucky Duck. A *Daily Sketch* reporter, pale and excited, raced through the bar like Paul Revere. "Redundancies in an hour. The management's drawing up the list. It's official, it's official."

Of course, we knew it couldn't be. The redundancies were not to be announced until Tuesday. The management had spoken. Besides, some of us had volunteered to go and that list was not even to be completed until Monday morning. Even so, the rumour was correct, in essence if not in detail. The announcement, we were told, would be made at seven o'clock and everyone would get a letter, whether he was redundant or not. Then the time was put back to nine o'clock and there would only be letters for those who had to go. Therefore we all had to hang around until nine and if, then, there was a letter for you, you were redundant and if there wasn't you weren't, unless, of course, your letter had been temporarily mislaid – by no means unlikely, it seemed to us, in the confusion that must be raging in the offices upstairs – in which case you might still be redundant and not know it.

The pub filled up, the different drinking groups mingling and intermingling in a way that would have been impossible under normal circumstances. A TV unit arrived to film our reactions in this fraught moment and a *Daily Mail* reporter, resenting its presence, took his trousers down in front of the camera. Behind me a handful of *Mail* men, drinking heavily though by no means drunk – indeed, despite the alcohol that was consumed that night I saw nobody drunk before the announcements were made, though plenty became so immediately afterwards – were composing a song about their predicament.

People joined the group I was with, stayed awhile and then wandered restlessly away. "You'll be all right," they said. "They'll never let you go."

"But I've volunteered," I said, meaninglessly. The fact of having volunteered could make no difference at all, since there was no way the management could know I had done so and yet it was a comfort somehow to know that my name was on that list.

"Yes but they won't accept that," people said. "They'll keep you." I wondered if they would and I wondered, too, how I would feel if they did. Disappointed, in a way, because I had long felt it

16

was time I left the *Mail* and yet probably relieved as well. Volunteering for redundancy was one thing; actually being without a job – a situation I had not been in for fifteen years – would undoubtedly be something else again.

More details filtered through of how the announcements were to be made. The heads of department were to be called in first, to be told their own future and given letters for the redundant ones on their staff. There was much speculation on what exactly would happen. Would somebody say, "You're fired. Oh, and on your way to the door, tell the others, will you?" My own position here was curious, if not unique. As a minor executive, more or less autonomous and not directly answerable to anyone except the editor, I had no idea who would tell me whether I was sacked or not. I had visions of myself wandering around the office throughout the night asking each executive I met whether he had a letter for me.

The atmosphere in the pub was remarkable. Everyone was laughing and joking; people were instructing Buck, the publican, to put bottles of champagne on the ice for later; but the groups kept changing, nobody could settle down and every now and then each member of each group would drop out of the conversation for a while and stop laughing and look thoughtful instead. One hundred and thirty-two people on the *Mail* were to be sacked, more than half the staff. "You'll be all right", people said to each other. "Yes, they'll keep you on." It was like polling night in a general election and each of us was a candidate in a marginal seat.

Just before nine we all started watching the clock, everyone eager to know the news and yet nobody wanting to seem too eager, too anxious, too frightened by being the first to return to the office. The composing group stopped singing, people ordered one more round and everyone drifted closer to the door.

I went back to the editorial floor about half-past nine. By then it was crowded with people waiting to discover their fate and there was very little laughter. Somebody said, "Christ, the whole back bench has gone." These men, the night executives, sat in a row at the head of the sub-editors' table and, one by one, the buzzers on their desks had rung and they had been called in to receive their letters. From the back of the room you could watch them falling like ten green bottles.

My own predicament – who was to tell me my news – was quickly solved. Through a mob of people I saw Iain Smith, the features editor, beckoning to me and in that moment I knew that he was out and so was I. "Would you go in and see Walter?" he said.

Walter Terry, the acting editor, was in the editor's office with a pile of envelopes and a list in front of him. I don't know how he was feeling but he looked very close to tears.

"I'm sorry," he said, "but I've got to give you one of these." And he handed me an envelope.

I said, fatuously, "That's all right, Walter." What can you say at such a time? I wanted to tell him that it didn't really matter because I'd volunteered anyway but it hardly seemed to be the moment, and I wanted to say something to ease his own pain but I couldn't think of anything.

He said, "It's not all right. You know it's not. It's bloody awful, bloody awful."

I walked out, waving my letter and smiling. It wasn't easy to smile, not because I felt bad (in truth, I didn't) but because I knew everyone would expect me to smile. The others who had been in before me were waiting in a group outside the editor's office and I showed my envelope to them. "Welcome to the club," said Geoff Bayliss, who, ten minutes before, had still been night editor.

At the other end of the room a group of friends, ignorant of their own fate, were waiting to see what had happened to me. "Well," they said, "are you in or out?" I waved my letter again. I still hadn't opened it; there was no point anyway because I knew what it contained.

"My God," said Sandy Fawkes, the fashion editor, "you look just like Chamberlain coming back from Munich."

Then the great mob of writers, reporters and photographers broke up as everyone rushed away to find the head of his department. I stood around holding my letter like a badge and people came up and showed me their letters and shook my hand and said, "Congratulations."

And then, while all this was going on, a magnificently Kafka-esque touch was added to the whole macabre situation.

A group of sightseers was being shown around the *Daily Mail* building and, with superb timing, they appeared on the editorial floor just as the redundancy notices were being distributed. One could imagine the guide saying, ". . . and this is where the famous *Daily Mail* writers work. In fact, if you look over the heads of the crowd you can see one of them hanging himself in the corner . . ."

Somebody rushed across to hustle them out and the rest of us were left to go about our private grief unobserved. We moved around the huge, crowded room comparing notes. One of the assistant editors was out; the features editor and his deputy were out; all the fe*Mail* staff bar one were out; all the foreign correspondents bar one were out; nearly all the feature writers were out.

The conversation was the same everywhere . . . "What about you, mate: in or out?"

"Out."

"Bad luck."

"Thanks, how about you?"

"I dunno. I haven't got a letter yet but I don't know. I just don't know."

The idea of 132 people being made redundant may not seem

much, but when those 132 people take human form and become your friends and colleagues it's appalling and heartless.

"Julian's out. And Olga. And Roy. And Pearson. And Tony. And Brian . . ."

"God Almighty, who's left?"

A features sub stood in the corridor and wept, not for himself, because he had been retained, but for his friends who had not. "John's out. And Bill. And Rhona. And Peter. And Sandy . . ."

The list seemed endless and illogical. Nearly all the people who, one had been sure, would be kept were in fact redundant – old people and young, men of long-service and short, the highly paid and the lowly. True, all the intellectuals and all those who might, by an effort of imagination, be considered intellectuals had been dismissed but otherwise there was no discernible pattern.

Down in the pub, a writer who had been retained, though he had wished to go, said "I think they've made a mistake. They've given the envelopes to the wrong people. They've kept all the bums and let the good ones go."

And indeed, even allowing for natural bias, it did begin to look as if the redundancy list had been drawn up by a man who couldn't tell Stork from butter.

In the office and the pub it was easy now to distinguish between those who had been fired and those who had not: the former were laughing and joking again, while the latter crept around with long and solemn faces as if they were walking on eggshells at a graveside.

There was no sign anywhere of either Arthur Brittenden, the retiring editor, or David English, the new one. Probably they were wise. Beneath all the mirth and euphoria there was an undercurrent of anger and it could, just, have been a little unsafe for anyone who might remotely have been considered a management man to show his face. Being made redundant is a strange, unmanning experience, even if you have volunteered for it. The sympathy and relief in the eyes of those who have been kept is very irritating and beyond that there is a sense of indignation that anyone could be fool enough to let you go. You wanted to go, of course, but God, what blind idiots they are actually to let you go . . .

"This is what you wanted, isn't it?" said a man at the bar. "Redundancy, I mean. You volunteered, didn't you?"

"Yes," I said. "Yes, I volunteered and yes, I want to go." And it was true enough. More news was coming now of the list of Ins and Outs at the *Daily Sketch* and it was possible to discern, if only dimly, the shape that the new *Daily Mail/Daily Sketch* would take.

"We're well out of it, mate," said a fellow-redundant. "It'll be like working for the *Daily Sketch* and you wouldn't like that."

No, indeed, I would not. I worked for the *Daily Sketch* a long time ago when I was a boy reporter and that's the right time to work for the *Daily Sketch*. It's no job for a grown man.

At 11.30 the pub closed and people, many of them very drunk now, went away clutching bottles of champagne and wine and spirits, either to take home to their wives, or to drink upstairs at impromptu parties on the editorial floor.

Outside, in the street, I met one of the senior sub-editors going home with his wife. "Are you out?" he asked. I said I was.

"You lucky bastard," he said. "They've kept me. I've just had a flaming row with Walter about it. I don't want to work for this bloody paper."

I sympathised with him. The *Daily Mail* may never have been a great newspaper but it has, at odd times, been a very good one and now, in all but name, it has vanished. Yes, I know that, officially, the *Mail* has absorbed the *Sketch* but it is the *Sketch* men who have taken nearly all the key posts. The spirit of the *Sketch*, as the paper itself declared a few days before the redundancies were announced, lives on.

"The man recovered of the bite. The dog it was that died."

A few weeks later, some time around the middle of May I suppose it was, I added a sequel to all that earlier stuff. Again, I haven't rewritten it; all I have done is to discard the précis of the last few pages which began it.

I thought, as I went home, that I should remember it all my life. And yet, a few days ago when someone asked me the exact date on which I became redundant, I had to look it up. I'd quite forgotten.

Strange things happen to you when you've been redunded – if there is such a word. First, there's a kind of euphoria – a sense of freedom, of release from bondage. A door has closed, yes, but surely there must be other doors to be marched up to and kicked open. One way of life has ended but only so that another may begin.

In my case this lasted a week or two. I was still going into the office, still going through the motions of working because we were not actually being released till the end of April. It was an exhilarating time, carefree and irresponsible, like the beginning of some endless holiday. Friends phoned me up and took me out for expensive lunches. Other friends suggested we should get together on various enterprises and I agreed, in principle, to them all – the good, the indifferent and the downright daft. In three days I agreed to collaborate on two books and two TV series none of which, I realised even then, was ever likely to come to anything.

It didn't matter. Who cared? I could do anything. Or nothing. I was free.

I'm not quite sure when the mood changed. Perhaps when I realised the office was divided into two camps – the Ins and the Outs.

The Ins were very nice to us Outs, treating us with grave consideration as if we were suffering from some incurable but honourable disease. And yet we were an embarrassment to them. They didn't really like having us around and I'm sure they wished we would go away. Our presence, I suppose, was an uncomfortable reminder that nobody is indispensable, that what had happened to us could as easily have happened to them.

Anyway, the euphoria died, to be replaced in my case by sloth and lethargy, a month of lotus-eating and gentle dreaming. I didn't now want to do anything at all. Oh, I knew there were things I had to do. I had work to find, a novel to write, a wife, two children, a pair of guinea pigs and a mortgage to support. But I didn't care about any of these things.

I still went into the office, attached now by a sort of umbilical cord. The office was a womb, a place of warmth and – oddly enough in the circumstances – of security. While I was there I didn't feel obliged to think of anything else – the future, for instance, or the money I should eventually have to earn, or even of my family.

I was aware of what was happening to me and vaguely dismayed by it. Every now and then I would examine myself for signs of physical and spiritual decay. In some ways this was reassuring. I hadn't taken to drink, though I was certainly smoking too much. I hadn't overnight become a wreck of the man I had once been. I wasn't even biting my fingernails.

But I wasn't doing other, more constructive things either. For some time, having a dread of growing fat, I'd been getting up early in the mornings and jogging two or three miles round the village. Now I abandoned that. It hardly seemed worth the bother of getting out of bed.

Again, until redundancy struck, I used to do a lot of writing at home, either in the mornings or the evenings. Now I gave that up, too. I watched TV instead – anything so long as it was bad and undemanding and there's quite a lot of that on TV. Over the weeks I took a kind of crash course in old B pictures, Westerns mainly. I sat there switching channels and watching Randolph Scott getting older every minute.

When television wasn't on I played cards or Scrabble with my young daughters. Anything to kill time. Because, for the first time in my life, I felt uncomfortable at home. Before, home had been my base and my refuge, the place to which I escaped with relief from the frustrations, irritations and idiocies of the office. But now I felt guilty and depressed there.

My time at home was my own and I should be using it to secure the future. I should be working. But I had neither the energy nor the desire to do so. In the evenings I felt sleepy and ready for bed even before the light had faded. At the weekends I welcomed every excuse to get out of the house.

I even welcomed the chance to work in the garden. This doesn't sound remarkable unless you know that the male members of my family have been renowned for several generations for their fierce and passionate lack of interest in gardening. This passion has reached its pinnacle in me. If there were a prize for the worst-kept garden in our village I could win it outright with no competition worth talking about. Even the other male members of my family look on the wreck of my garden with considerable awe. The lawn is like an unploughed field; the few flowers hide coyly beneath the nettles and the cow parsley; the fruit trees grope wildly in all directions, unpruned and uncared for.

Yet now I was deeply upset when the mower wouldn't work.

To compensate I spent hours digging up weeds, lighting bonfires, carting loads of topsoil about, creating flowerbeds in the wilderness and planning new stretches of lawn. Incredibly, I even enjoyed this work. It kept me from thinking and it kept me on my own. I didn't have to talk to anybody.

Because now, too, I wanted to avoid my friends. At first I welcomed them when they sympathised or offered gruff encouragement – "Best thing that could have happened to you. You were in a rut at the *Mail*. You needed a shake-up." In many ways it was true. I agreed with them. But I no longer wanted to discuss it with them. I would rather cross the street than face the sympathy of a friend.

In any case, I wasn't quite like them any more. I was redundant and they weren't. I was different: not inferior, just different. After all, what does redundancy mean? It doesn't mean you've been fired because your work is no good. On the contrary. Everyone, even the chairman, was careful to say that there was no reflection whatsoever on one's ability, loyalty, energy, dedication or any of the other things that managements find so desirable in their employees. No, I and others had been kicked out for no other reason than that the firm couldn't afford to employ us any more.

It's a misty, unreal kind of feeling. You've done nothing at all to deserve the sack and yet you've been sacked. The quality of your work is unquestioned but your employer doesn't want you.

Curiously enough, there was no sense of shame involved as there would have been, I suppose, if I'd been fired for robbing the till or beating up the editor or improperly assaulting the chairman's wife. And at the same time I can honestly say that I felt no sense of grievance nor resentment either.

Nor did I envy those who were staying on. I didn't really want to stay but on the other hand I didn't really want to go. I simply didn't want to take decisions or face responsibilities. I just wanted to drift.

A man who has been laid off – and what a bleak, dreary phrase that is – exists in a kind of limbo which can only be properly understood by others who have been laid off, too. The strongest emotion he feels – or at least that I felt – is a mild bewilderment. In a way I was happy enough to go – time for a change and that sort of thing – but, oh dear, what fools they were actually to let me go, still less insist upon it.

I honestly had no idea what set of circumstances had led to my being among the 50 per cent released rather than the 50 per cent retained. Perhaps my kind of writing wouldn't fit the new paper. Or perhaps my face wouldn't fit. Perhaps I was too highly paid for the budget. Perhaps they drew the names out of a hat, or left it to a computer, or someone ran through the staff list saying "eeny-meeny-mini-mo". I don't know. Nobody told me and I didn't ask. I didn't really care, although sometimes I wondered about it in an idle way.

It didn't matter anyway. Nothing mattered. Well, no, that's not quite true. The loss of identity bothered me a bit, the sense of not belonging anywhere any more, of being just me instead of me of the *Daily Mail*.

But I didn't actually lose any sleep over it. If the thought began to worry me I simply turned back to Randolph Scott, the oldest gun in the West, who, comfortingly, seemed always to be on the telly.

In this strange and not very pleasant period there was one great consolation and that was my wife's attitude. Somehow, though I didn't talk about it, she understood what was going on. She didn't urge me to work or go out and find a job. She just left me alone to sort it all out for myself.

And I think now that I have sorted it out. Or at least I'm beginning to. I've got some work to do – not a lot but enough. A start anyway. I'm thinking about my novel again, plotting and planning and scheming for the future again, looking for those new doors which I must kick down or bash in or at least knock politely upon.

Of course there will still be bad times. I don't, for instance, think my bank manager is going to be deliriously happy about the way my income drops this year. Come to that, I'm not too crazy about it myself. But it'll be okay. Eventually.

At least the lethargy has gone and that sense of detachment from the rest of the world. I may still be out of steady, full-time work but, thank God, I don't feel redundant any more.

1
Of birds and bees and men and women and other horrid things

The Sex War

The last time I saw Richard Burton we were in Milan and drinking vodka and he said, "Tell me something – do you like women?"

"Yes," I said, careless of what other men might think of me. "Yes, I do."

"You do?" he said, his voice rising on a note of incredulity.

"Yes."

"You really like women?"

"Yes," I said. "I really like women."

"Holy Christ!" said Mr Burton.

Now I don't know what caused this strange outburst, nor do I feel that we should read too much into it. The conversation took place in the early part of this year and there's a very fair chance that, at the time, Mr Burton was having a little local difficulty with his old lady, the motherly Elizabeth Taylor. It's quite possible, for I have no wish to be unfair to the man, that had I caught him on another day and in another mood his attitude would have been entirely different.

In any event, let us now forget Richard Burton for he has no further bearing on the matter in hand. The point is that the snatch of dialogue quoted above reflects what I believe to be a general truth: namely, that most men don't like women.

They desire women, fancy women, are turned on by women, touch women, stroke women, goose women, grope women, lay women and sometimes even love women. But they don't actually like them.

The truth of this is pretty obvious and, indeed, the evidence is all around us. For a start there's the girlie-mag syndrome – all those beaming, curvaceous, lifeless, bloodless nudes, girls who neither sweat nor belch, nor eat garlic, nor ever have holes in their tights. Even their pubes appear to have been attacked by someone skilled in the topiary art.

Ostensibly, of course, these centre-fold spreads are a hymn of praise to women, a glorification of the feminine gender but in fact they are the very opposite.

These are not real women. Women in their naked state they may be – but they're not women in their natural state. They're women who have been arranged and groomed and draped and posed and cunningly lit and virtually manufactured by men to resemble, as far as possible, lifesized foam-rubber dolls such as one might be able to buy (should one's tastes run in such a direction) from the back room of some enterprising porn shop.

To the casual onlooker the effect of these girlie studies is merely to stimulate a mild erotic fantasy. But if you look at them more closely you realise that while the male observer is being invited to say "Cor!" and pant a little, he is also being invited, rather subtly, to feel contempt for women.

All those *Playboy* Playmates and *Penthouse* Pets – the very names are an insult – are actually a total put-down of women.

For example, a recent *Playboy* cover showed an extraordinarily pretty girl lying, face down, on a couch. She was wearing stockings and some kind of shift and her buttocks (buttocks, I may add, that were a joy to behold) were bare. The whole pose suggested mild depravity and also utter humiliation. This, the picture hinted, was how women ought to be – lewd and vulnerable and degraded for the benefit of rampant, virile man.

Well, all right, to anyone who has made even a casual study of the continuing conflict between man and women, this is kindergarten stuff. But it's worth repeating, I think, because the girlie mag is the clearest example of the ambivalent attitude of the male towards the female – hostility thinly disguised as lust. What's more, its influence spreads.

Perhaps you've noticed the way women are treated in films. Once upon a time they were all virgins like Doris Day, untouchable creatures moving across the silver screen with, as it were, their knees together and their hand on their ha'penny. For much of the time, as the plot unfolded, woman was on a pedestal, a lofty being usually wooed by and about to wed some dreadful, wet, namby-pamby intellectual manifestly not good enough for her.

But then, with about five minutes to go before the end credits, someone like John Wayne grabbed hold of her, put her across his knee, smacked her bottom and thus earned her undying devotion.

Slow fade on Wayne striding manfully out of town with the once cool but now suitably cowed lady running after him shouting, "Wait for me, Dook!"

Well, that was bad enough. But now things are decidedly worse. Women in contemporary films must, if they're under forty, automatically expect to strip or be stripped naked. They're portrayed as sluts and whores and very often they're beaten up and raped, frequently in a gang-bang. Men don't get stripped or raped or gang-banged but then the people who write, produce and direct these films, it hardly needs to be said, are men.

Still, the fact that purveyors of soft-core porn and a good many film-makers don't like women hardly justifies, by itself, the argument that men in general don't like women either. So, okay, let's look for evidence farther afield.

Let's take the State. The State is masculine, right? Women like Shirley Williams and Barbara Castle and Margaret Thatcher may come and go, tentatively and uneasily established in high office and brief authority (usually in some impossible area like labour relations, consumer affairs and education) but the State is essentially masculine. The Government and the Civil Service are run by men, the law is created and dispensed by men with the occasional token lady judge or magistrate perched uncomfortably on a bench.

Now Parliament will, from time to time, debate with owlish wisdom Bills and Acts to give women equal rights and, with some reluctance, they will even pass such Bills and Acts.

But this is simply lip-service, a small bone thrown to a section of the community which, though essentially negligible, is potentially bothersome because it happens to be just about in the majority and, through some aberration in the past, even has the vote.

So, in theory, the masculine State says that women are equal. But what does the State say in practice? It says that the foreign-born wife of a British male is automatically British, while the foreign-born husband of a British female is automatically foreign. Can anyone really believe that the State likes women?

Yet hold on a moment. All this loose talk about women and we haven't even defined the creature yet. What, in the view of man, is a woman? Well, a woman is "an animal that micturates once a day, defecates once a week, menstruates once a month, parturates once a year and copulates whenever she gets the opportunity". Somerset Maugham said that but we all know about *him*, don't we, so perhaps we ought to make allowances.

But then Kipling said a woman was "a rag and a bone and a hank of hair", and he also said "a woman is only a woman but a good cigar is a smoke". Even Shakespeare, most perceptive of men, trotted out "frailty thy name is woman", while Byron who had at least his share of women, God knows, and should have known better, once remarked ". . . as soon seek roses in December . . . believe a woman or an epitaph or any other thing that's false . . ."

Shakespeare again – Ophelia: " 'Tis brief, my Lord"; Hamlet: "As woman's love". And Pope: "Men, some to business, some to pleasure take; But every woman is at heart a rake." And Thomas Otway: "Destructive, damnable, deceitful woman!" And John Gay: "So he that tastes woman, woman, woman, He that tastes woman, ruin meets." And that sixteenth-century double act of Beaumont and Fletcher: "There is no other purgatory but a woman." And Ecclesiasticus: "All wickedness is but little to the wickedness of a woman." And Meredith: "I expect that Woman will be the last thing civilized by Man."

Even Walter Scott's apparent cry of devotion: "O Woman! in our hours of ease, Uncertain, coy and hard to please, And variable as the shade, By the light, quivering aspen made; When pain and anguish wring the brow, A ministering angel thou!" – even that has a sardonic touch to it. Note the exclamation mark at the end, the literary equivalent of a mocking tongue thrust into the cheek.

I could go on. Literature is full of derogatory remarks made by man against women but by now, surely, the point has been established. Almost everywhere you look man's distaste for women becomes evident and this is a state of affairs that has existed since time began.

It was, you will recall, a silly, randy woman who got us all kicked out of the Garden of Eden with the wielder of the boot yelling: "And stay out!" Perhaps man never forgave her for that. Certainly, as time went by, hostility became more and more obvious.

Pretty early on, St Paul laid it on the line. Even if she wasn't actually unclean woman wasn't fit to bare her head in church, still less to raise her voice. "Let your women keep silence in the churches," said St Paul, doubtless chewing the fat with the lads over a glass of communion wine, "for it is not permitted unto them to speak."

And then, just to make sure everyone got the message, he said it again: "If they will learn any thing, let them ask their husbands at home: for it is a shame for women to speak in the church."

To this day the churches believe that. Women are all right to clean the brass, sweep the aisles, make the crosses for Palm Sunday, decorate the manger for Christmas mass and, occasionally and under strict supervision, to read a Lesson. But where in the Church of England, or most other churches for that matter, are your lady archbishops, cardinals, rabbis, canons, rectors or even curates?

Well, let us, at this stage, assume that I've made my point. Most men don't like women. The question, therefore, to be asked is: why? The answer, I have to confess, is not quickly to be found but then I speak as one who does like women – a pompous statement which, if interpreted uncharitably, might even appear condescending. Nevertheless, it's true: I do like women. I'd rather have dinner with a woman any time than spend a night out with the boys.

And if I qualify this by adding that, even more, I'd rather have dinner with a *pretty* woman then, all right, deplorable though it may be, the last vestiges of male chauvinist piggery clearly linger on.

The fact is, however, that I'm in a minority. The average man of my acquaintance – and yours, if you're honest – would rather get drunk with his mates than chat up a girl by himself.

Now, what's the reason for this? Do men find it difficult to talk to women? Yes, they do as a matter of fact – largely because their natural suspicion and uneasiness makes them regard women as a special breed who have to be spoken to in a special way. Most men find it difficult to talk to children, too, and for the same reason.

What they fail to realise is that women and children, like other men, react best when they're spoken to simply as human beings. Yet the average man, finding himself in the frightful position of being alone with a strange woman, immediately thinks: "Oh, my God, I've got to talk to this girl and I don't know anything about babies or shopping or fashion or . . . What the hell am I going to say?"

It would never occur to him to say, as he might to another man, "What do you think about the bloody Government/Northern Ireland/Watergate/the England football team *now* then?"

But if he did he might well find that the wary, slightly bored creature sitting opposite, who has already been given a considerable pain in the arse by other men asking her about babies, shopping and fashion, would suddenly become animated, articulate, intelligent, thoughtful and extremely attractive.

I suppose it all goes back to childhood, education and the home environment. Little girls and little boys are treated differently from the start. Little girls are petted and cossetted and given soft, cuddly toys to play with.

Little boys (even if they're not sent sternly off to boarding school at the age of eight, thus being effectively cut off from all feminine company until it's too late) are given guns and soldiers and encouraged to climb trees and kick footballs – whether they want to or not – and are told that only little girls and cissies cry.

Consequently little boys grow up in the naïve belief that they are superior beings and, to their eternal discredit, little girls are often guilty of encouraging them in this delusion.

There's still a strong school of thought which urges the girl who wishes to get her man to hide her intelligence, to ask him questions even when she knows the answers better than he does and never to contradict him when he trots out a load of mindless rubbish masquerading as information.

Daisy in *The Great Gatsby* wanted her daughter to be "an empty-headed, beautiful fool" because she knew perfectly well that empty-headed, beautiful fools are what men like best.

What men like least, of course, are clever women who don't mind admitting they're clever. I know a girl who was once employed in market research – a most attractive girl with an honours degree and trained in mathematics, philosophy and logic. One of her tasks was to make a regular report to a meeting of the company executives, all of them men, and she hated it.

As soon as she appeared they would gambol around her like Labrador puppies, red-faced, hearty and ponderously flirtatious. One can imagine the scene . . . Nudge, nudge, wink, wink. "Bags I sit next to Jenny" and an arm thrust awkwardly round her waist, hugging her till she squeaked, while the other men stood by admiringly and said: "Look at old Charles – a devil with the women."

I asked her once what would have happened had she grabbed old Charles with well-simulated passion and she said, regretfully, that she'd never thought of it but it would probably have worked: he'd have been so terrified that he would never have spoken to her again.

What annoyed her most, though, was that they treated her report as a joke.

It was their defence mechanism against the enemy. If ever they had admitted that this alien being was not only prettier than they but at least as intelligent they would have been unmanned and destroyed.

Much easier for them to paraphrase Dr Johnson and kid themselves that a woman in market research was like a dog walking on its hind legs – "it is not done well; but you are surprised to find it done at all".

And, indeed, one *is* surprised to find it done at all. It's not so very long since people believed that girls didn't need educating; a bit of shorthand and typing to tide them over until they got married and that was enough. Even now, when education for girls is grudgingly admitted to be a good thing, the kind of education they are offered is limited.

If they get to university at all (and the proportion of female to male undergraduates is conspicuously low) they are shoved firmly towards art courses, which qualify them mostly to be teachers, teaching being a profession so ill-paid as to be suitable only for women.

But how many female graduates are there in chemistry, physics and engineering? And of those few graduates how many are employed in jobs where they can actually use their knowledge and their degrees?

Woman then, particularly intelligent woman, is a threat and that brings us to the whole nub of man's dislike for her, which is fear. Woman is not only a dangerous adversary who, in argument, employs unfair weapons like tears and icy silences and whom you can't decently curse or hit as you might a man, she is also a mystery.

She has strange bodily functions which the average man neither understands nor wishes to understand. She bleeds and gives birth and gives suck and other unnatural things.

Worst of all, she is more potent than man. In matters of sex she can keep going, lustfully and joyously, long after he has collapsed into slumber – a spent force. So a woman, no matter how desirable, arouses in a man doubts and fears as to his prowess and virility. And in an age when the pressure of modern life is rendering more and more men more and more impotent, the frustration man feels at finding the flesh unable to perform what the spirit wills turns into rage against woman. Okay, it's his quest for money and power that has robbed him of his virility but he's not doing all this for himself, is he? Good heavens, no – he's doing it for her. So, in effect, she is the one who has emasculated him.

In any case, sex is the real cause of all the trouble. Men have never truly felt happy about sex. It was old St Paul again (a fellow who has much to answer for) who said, "It is a good thing for a man to have nothing to do with women", and man has believed that, if only sub-consciously, ever since.

He is conditioned to believe that sex is a furtive, surreptitious act, something bestial and unclean that, while he is engaged in it, robs him of all defence and dignity. When it is finished he is overcome by post-coital remorse.

Why did he perform this sweaty, grunting deed? Why? Well, because of woman, of course, woman the traditional temptress, arousing his primitive desires, preying on his weakness.

It's hateful – but whom to hate? Not himself, surely. Wasn't his fault, was it? She egged him on, didn't she? Had it not been for her, wicked, odious creature, this could never have happened. So there's his scapegoat – at the same time both the culprit and, as it were, the scene of the crime.

It could be – and I hope it may prove so – that all this is changing. More coeducation and a growing conviction, particularly among the young, that men and women aren't really so very different, despite all appearances to the contrary, should eventually bring about a truce and possibly peaceful coexistence between the sexes.

But for the present most men don't like women and just at the moment women aren't helping them a lot to change their minds. Women's Lib must take its share of responsibility for this – and so must magazines like *Cosmopolitan* with their appeal to a liberated, independent, self-confident and even aggressive woman. Men don't merely dislike women like that – men *hate* women like that, because such women frighten them abominably.

Men are timid creatures really and all the vociferous femininity around these days is bringing them to the conclusion that women don't like *them* very much. Maybe that's true. I wouldn't know, though no doubt you can tell me.

Meanwhile, what is true, and is likely to remain so for some time, is that most men would be inclined to take their motto from Lord Kitchener's advice to the troops in 1914 – "while treating all women with perfect courtesy, you should avoid any intimacy". Well, not *any* intimacy perhaps but you know what I mean. Don't trust the devils.

From Cosmopolitan
November, 1974

I include the following because it happens to be the first piece I ever wrote for The Guardian. *I'd been asked by Alastair Hetherington to take a few days thinking about whether I'd like to write leaders for him and then come in with my decision. I'd actually decided I couldn't do it, being far too ignorant, and had gone in to tell him so but before I could say a word I was ushered into the full* Guardian *leader writers' conference. One by one they went through their ideas: the significance of the latest Sino-Russian détente, the economic plight of Bulgaria, the lessons to be learnt from the recent troop movements in the Sinai desert . . . And then it came to my turn. "Any ideas?" said Alastair Hetherington. I was too panic-stricken to tell him what I'd really come in to say. "Well," I said, "there's, you know, well, I mean, there's this bit about Women's Lib and the Mafia and, you know, like that . . ." The other leader writers, the* real *leader writers, looked at me in polite astonishment as well they might. "All right," said Alastair Hetherington. "Have a go at it. We'll see what it's like . . ."*

A Little Feminine Enterprise

To keep in the vanguard of Women's Lib today a girl has to be quite remarkably inventive. It is worth noting that such girls are still around and active. In Sardinia, for instance – a place not much associated with liberated women – a housewife took a firm step in the right direction by locking her husband in a chastity belt whenever he left the house. It was, she said, to stop him getting lewd ideas about other women; or anyway to stop him putting those ideas into practice. The husband complained, understandably, of embarrassment. He felt such a fool, he said, as he clanked noisily about the streets. Worse, his wife accused him of being impotent, as well he might be, thus encumbered. A merciful judge ordered his release from these fetters but nevertheless the point had been made and, we may be sure, duly noted that what is sauce for the goose goes very nicely with the gander, too.

Yet for the most dramatic example of the new woman we must look to Sicily where, it has been revealed or at least alleged, the gym mistress of a convent school has become the first woman boss in Mafia history. Great heavens, is nothing sacred? Frails muscling in on the mob yet, bringing with them no doubt their implacable domestic touch, dusting and polishing probably between heists, converting the whole operation into a kind of Cosy Nostra. The prospect is enough to cause veteran Mafiosi to weep into their bootleg hooch and confide, brokenly, to each other that the world has grown so bad that wrens do prey where eagles fear to perch.

To outsiders, however, the lady's achievement is a splendid example of feminine enterprise. Hollywood will certainly welcome it. A whole new wave of gangster movies will probably burst upon us: *Scarface Alice Capone*, perhaps, or *The Rise and Fall of Lucy Luciano*. And all thanks, in a way to Women's Lib.

Guardian *Leader Column*
July 17, 1971

Six Mislaid in Transit

To lose one parent, as Lady Bracknell observed, may be regarded as a misfortune; to lose both looks like carelessness. Much the same might be said of Prince Abdul Aziz Elpheni of Saudi Arabia who mislaid his entire harem the other day at Orly Airport. To lose one concubine is the sort of rotten luck that could happen to any of us; to lose six (which he achieved by dashing away to his private coach, leaving them behind) shows a degree of carelessness verging on the blasé. Luckily for him they were discovered, bundled together, and as is the way with abandoned baggage, left outside the terminal.

Otherwise he might have had some awkward moments at the lost property office . . . "I see, sir. Six concubines, you say. Well, we might have them and there again we might not. Could you describe them for us?" Not an easy task that, even with hands etching shapes in the air and such incidental information as, "well, a dark girl with big – I might even say very big – well, you know . . ." How many men could provide a recognisable description of their own wives, let alone a whole harem of sort-of-wives?

Other problems might have arisen, too. Were they insured, for instance? And for how much? And what proportion of the sum would the insurance company have withheld for wear and tear? "Now, sir, you've had this one for four years. Well, she may have been worth 14 camels and 28 sheep when you acquired her. But after four years can you honestly say . . .?"

Equally fascinating is the question of where responsibility lay for the initial loss. If with the Prince, well and good. But if with the airline, then what? Would they have had to replace the missing articles? Difficult if the originals had been a matched set. The best solution, possibly, would have been to offer six nearly new air hostesses in exchange.

No, perhaps best and safest of all might be for the Prince to leave his valuables at home when travelling. If friends remarked on their absence he could always say he had been advised to cut down.

Guardian *Leader Column*
August 13, 1971

Abreast of the Times

Do you, asked a question posed by delegates to the Royal Society of Health Congress and paraphrased rather neatly in a newspaper report, feel exploited by advertisers, worried about euthanasia and abortion or obsessed with big breasts?

When you think about it, that's a pretty crafty list because just about everybody's hang-up must be in there somewhere. Speaking for myself, I'm not too bothered about advertisers, while, with any luck, euthanasia is unlikely to be visited upon me yet awhile and the possibility of my undergoing an abortion is fairly remote.

No, doctor, it's the big breasts that get me. I don't mean commercially exploited breasts, either – not the globular, foam-rubber breasts beckoning chastely from the pages of *Playboy*, nor even the breasts that dreamt they flew to the moon in their Maidenhead bra.

I mean to say, there they are – honest breasts earning an honest crust, steady hardworking breasts that one can look upon, dispassionately, as colleagues in the rat race.

Nor do I refer to the secretary breasts and housewife breasts that press menacingly upon me in rush-hour bus and Tube, so that I stand, hands in pockets like an armless man, hopping from foot to foot in a pathetic balancing act, fearing even to reach for the overhead rail or strap, lest I should miss and inadvertently grab instead . . . No, no, it hardly bears thinking about.

But the breasts that really worry me (and here, doctor I'd like your considered opinion) are the cocky, free-thinking breasts of Women's Lib, undisciplined and untrammelled by underbodice or *soutien-gorge*. They've not been seen about much lately because, after all, it has been rather chilly but any moment now they'll be bursting forth to disturb me again.

Am I, I ask myself as they point the stern nipple of accusation, doing enough for these poor, oppressed, freedom-seeking breasts? The answer, alas, is no. Wrapped in my cocoon of male chauvinist piggery, I watch them, doomed but gallant, demonstrating at the offices of *Punch* and in the masculine sanctuary of El Vino's and I do nothing.

Well, I do a bit. I haunt the escalators at Tube stations, scrawling "This advertisement exploits breasts" over the bras and bikini-tops. But is that enough, doctor? Will it finally rid me of my obsession and let me devote my thoughts, in peace, to the problems of euthanasia?

May 1, 1972

Snap, Crackle and Bop!

Miss Barbara Cartland, with the aid of Messrs Hutchinson, has produced a *Book of Etiquette*, full of useful information about how to address one's butler (by his surname) and one's boot-boy (by his first name). I mention this because, if your butler's been a bit stroppy lately, you'll know it's on account of your calling him Ernie instead of Postlethwaite.

However, Miss Cartland also has other snappy advice to offer, much of it about manners in marriage, which is all very well for newly-weds but strikes me as rather dangerous if adopted without prior warning by old hands at the game. Consider the following breakfast-time scene:

"Thank you, darling."

"What?"

"I said, 'Thank you, darling'. For the breakfast, you know. Hang on a bit while I shave and I'll give you a kiss as well."

"What have you been up to?"

"I haven't been up to anything!"

"Yes, you have. You've never said thank you for a bowl of cornflakes in your life. And you haven't bothered to shave before kissing me since that ludicrous seduction scene the night we got engaged. Why are you being so nice to me? You've got another bird, haven't you, you rat!"

"No, of course I haven't! It's just that Barbara Cartland says . . ."

"So that's it! You're having an affair with Barbara Cartland. My God!"

"Don't be ridiculous! I don't even know Barbara Cartland . . ."

"Of course! That explains everything. I wondered why you phoned me that night I went to visit my mother. It was to make sure I was out of the way, wasn't it?"

"No! I just wanted to know that you'd arrived safely. Barbara Cartland says . . ."

"Aha. She put you up to it, did she? I might have known. You rotten, sneaky, lousy . . . Oh, it's all becoming clear to me now. That's why you object to my opening your mail all of a sudden, isn't it? She's been writing to you!"

"No, she hasn't! It's just that Barbara Cartland says marriage partners should never open each other's letters . . ."

"I *bet* she does! She's been sending you bloody perfumed *billets-doux*, hasn't she? Well, I'll show you, mate!"

"Ethel, if you throw those cornflakes I'll . . . Aargh!"

"And tell that to Barbara Cartland next time you sneak off and meet her, though what she sees in a bald, unshaven, fat, paunchy wreck like you I'll never know."

"Ethel, I hope you realise this is the end of our marriage?"

"You bet your life it is, baby! You and Barbara Cartland . . ."

October 30, 1972

This piece was inspired by the strenuous efforts of Mrs Whitehouse to have Chuck Berry's naughty but innocuous little song, "My Ding-a-ling" banned from the airwaves . . .

Mary Tidings

Thanks to the courageous intervention of Mrs Mary Whitehouse that truly filthy song, "Jingle Bells" has been permanently banned from radio and television.

Subversive, and no doubt Communist-inspired, elements within the BBC were planning to give it several airings over the Christmas period, with the cynical intention of spreading its moral pollution among the young.

Fortunately, however, at the eleventh hour news of this dastardly plot was delivered, along with a copy of the sheet music, to Mrs Whitehouse, who immediately got on the job or, to put it another way, sprang into action, by which I mean she made an urgent reverse-charge call to Lord Hill at Broadcasting House.

The opening lyrics of the song – "Jingle bells, jingle bells, jingle all the way" – had been enough to convince her that this was not merely an open incitement to self- and mutual-masturbation, but an open incitement to permanent, day-long, marathon self- and mutual-masturbation, probably indulged in, what's more, while travelling.

If this were not enough, an even more corrupting line appeared later in the verse, to wit: "Oh, what fun it is to ride in a one-horse open sleigh." Well, of course, we all know what *that* means, and if we don't Mrs Whitehouse does and naturally she wishes to put a stop to it at once.

Encouragement to people to engage in orgiastic behaviour in one-horse open sleighs is, as she announced in a press release, calculated to destroy the moral fibre of the nation. Furthermore, it could very easily frighten the horses.

Lord Hill, who it is alleged claimed sanctuary with the head of Religious Broadcasting as soon as he learnt it was Mrs Whitehouse on the phone again, said in a statement later that he was quite sure she must be right, though heaven alone knew where she got her ideas from and why couldn't she get off his back, and thank God he was retiring soon and wouldn't have to put up with all this rubbish much longer.

Meanwhile, Mrs Whitehouse is reported to be turning her attention to that equally masturbatory song, "Ding Dong Merrily on High", which, she said, clearly exhorts people to practise unnatural acts on chandeliers.

In addition she has instructed Scotland Yard to mount, or anyway to instigate, a series of rigorous raids on the music shops of Tin Pan Alley where, she has been informed, depraved people may buy in plain covers copies of a work of hard-core pornography, blatantly entitled, "Oh, Come, All Ye Faithful".

December 4, 1972

Stark Company

In the interests of Men's Lib I am here to say that there will be no

all-nude playboy calendars in my house next year, thank you very much.

Apart from anything else I really don't think I could face the prospect of coming down to breakfast and finding a full-frontal meat porter with a side of pork over his shoulder glowering seductively at me above the Zodiac sign for Aries, the ram.

There are some things that the delicate human stomach should not be asked to contemplate first thing in the morning and full-frontal meat porters rate pretty high among them. So, for the matter of that and lest anyone should accuse me of harbouring a class-conscious prejudice against naked meat porters, do full-frontal dentists, bank clerks, stockbrokers, property speculators and High Court judges, bewigged or otherwise.

However, as you will obviously appreciate, it's not simply the aesthetic considerations that call forth my objection to the present influx on to the market of nude-male calendars.

Nor is it the fact that nobody has asked me to pose for one – although you'd think they would, wouldn't you? After all, the *Sun* got Michael Parkinson to strip to the navel (from above, I imagine he'd like me to add), so I shouldn't have thought it was too much to expect, say *The Nursing Mirror*, to make me at least a tentative offer.

If I took a deep breath and held my tummy in I reckon I'd look quite as nice as Michael Parkinson and the fact that I've not been approached only serves to emphasise the deplorable decline in female taste.

Not, of course, that I would dream of accepting. Unlike a certain Mr Taylor in the latest of these calendars – and there are now at least two on the market, one with the utterly shrivelling title of *The Ladies Home Companion* – you won't find me posing, coy and starkers, over the open bonnet of a car. (A very dangerous procedure in any case, I should have thought, for an unwary lad, when you consider the damage that a swiftly revolving fan belt might cause.)

No, had one of the young women who hustled up models for their calendar accosted me in the street and told me how nice I would look without my clothes on, I knew precisely how I should have reacted.

I cannot, naturally, speak for anyone else. Some men, in a similar situation, would, I expect, mutter despairingly from the corners of their mouths, "Oh, not now, darling, the missus is watching." Others would probably say, "Give me your phone number and we'll talk it over at my flat", while yet others, I shouldn't be surprised, would simply fall upon their interlocutors with hoarse, gutteral cries and pursue them for several blocks.

At least one, apparently, actually agreed to pose as requested and then persuaded his mother to give him £50 to change his mind, thus indicating to me that here is a young fellow to watch and one who will certainly end up rich.

If I, however, had been propositioned as were the craven traitors to their sex who appear on the most recent calendar, I should at once have exclaimed "How dare you!" and struck the hussy with my shoulder bag.

Because – and here we come to the whole crux of the matter – what is so offensive about these calendars (as equally about those advertisements on Underground stations in which a group of the boys sit around the locker-room chatting in their pastel-coloured Y-fronts) is the way they typify the wicked and continuing exploitation of men.

Women are only after one thing, you know. What are we chaps to them but just so many sexual toys and playthings?

You only have to watch them in crowded buses and trains, stripping us with their eyes, mentally and lewdly divesting us of our braces, waistcoats, chest protectors and thermal underwear as we sit there innocently studying the financial pages, to know what hot, seething images whirl about their lustful heads and what deep animal passions beat in their bra-less breasts.

It's our bodies they want, that's all. Why can't they love us for our minds? Some of us may not, to tell the truth, be all that much to write home about in the body line but we have awfully nice minds.

Women don't care about that, though. Ask any woman which she would sooner have – a picture of Mr Taylor naked and leaning over his open car bonnet or a nice, tasteful portrait of Mr Norman St John-Stevas and see what answer you get. Female chauvinist sows.

December 11, 1972

Blues in the Night

America appears, yet again, to be in the throes of a sexual crisis and so, for that matter, does Rome. In Rome, an increase in male impotence has been attributed to the traffic noise and I can well believe it.

The sudden crash of gears, blare of horns, exchange of wild oaths, and deafening thunk of cars colliding head-on outside the window could easily take a sensitive man's mind off other things.

In America, matters are even worse. Psychiatrists there talk gravely of "the new impotence" and "the crisis of masculinity", the sexual decline of the man in the grey flannel suit and the corresponding rise of the blue-collar lover.

What has happened, apparently, is that middle-class American woman, having so belaboured middle-class American man that he is fit for nothing save amassing wealth and dying betimes of a coronary, has now turned her insatiable attentions to working-class American man.

In a magazine article of terrifying candour, middle-class intellectual women have extolled the virtues of the blue-collared lover who has "a raw, prole strength" in contrast to the "lily white, endlessly verbal men, out of shape and driven, sapped up and leeched out by mental work, always threatened and so tense".

One such woman bragged of her conquest of a truck driver who wore white socks in bed; another spoke of her three blue-collar husbands, "all violent, brutish and short".

A third advertised the "joys and perils of taking your taxi driver home to bed"; a fourth maintained that "blue-collar men and relaxed millionaires are the only good lovers".

Little wonder, then, that a *Time* magazine writer, quite unable to compete, publicly confessed his own loss of potency and rushed off to the South Sea islands on the off-chance that somebody may have handed it in there.

One might say, of course, well, that's America and Rome – it couldn't happen here. The point is that it could happen here and actually I think it's happened already.

For instance, now I understand why I can never find a taxi late at night. All the drivers have been whipped away by famished middle-class women in search of joys and perils and are lying around in their white socks, violent, brutish, and short, and quite likely petrified out of their minds.

(Incidentally, I can imagine what the joys are but I'm not so sure about those unspecified perils – unless avaricious taxi drivers leave their meters running and charge double fares for extra-curricular duties after midnight.)

In the face of such aggressive feminine over-drive one doesn't know whom to feel sorrier for – emasculated middle-class man or exploited blue-collar worker. (Relaxed millionaires we need not bother about. To hell with relaxed millionaires.)

But it'll be hard for people like milkmen and dustmen, traditional prey of mad dogs, if they are now to be faced by another occupational hazard in the shape of voracious, middle-class housewives . . .

"Mornin', lady, I was just wonderin' . . ."

"Wonder no more, you great hunk of raw prole strength! Cummere."

"Eh? 'Ere, no, you got the wrong bloke, lady. It's the relief milkman you're after. He's the Prole. Come over from Proland just after . . ."

"Shut the door and don't talk. Whatever else, don't talk! God, if you knew how sick I am of lily white, endlessly verbal men, out of shape and driven, sapped up and leeched out by mental work, always threatened and so tense."

"What? Look, lady, I only wanted to ask . . ."

"Ask, ask – and the answer is Yes, oh, yes! You look violent, brutish, and short. Are you? Are you violent, brutish, and short?"

"Me? I dunno, lady. I only wanted . . ."

"Say no more – I shall see to your wants! Do you wear white socks in bed? Have you ever known the joys and perils of taking your taxi driver . . ."

"'Ello, what was that? I swear I heard someone say, 'Stop that bloody noise!'"

"Yes – my husband. He's in the dining-room, trying to get his potency back. It's quieter there, you see. Tell me, did you know that blue-collar workers and relaxed millionaires are the only . . ."

"I dunno what your game is, lady, but do you want . . ."

"Yes! I want, I want!"

"Blimey, thank Gawd we got that straight. Two cartons or one?"

"Pardon?"

"Yoghurt. I'm asking about yoghurt. Two cartons or one?"

Too much of this kind of thing and it won't just be *Time* magazine writers who dash off to the South Seas in search of their potency. We'll all be there, blue-collared or white, forming a queue. Indeed, I'd like to say to that *Time* magazine man: if you see some unclaimed virility lying about the Lost Potency Office, tell them it's mine, will you?

February 26, 1973

Starlet Nights

"See that girl?" said the man on the terrace of the Carlton Hotel at Cannes. "Six hundred francs, she is."

"Pardon?" I said.

"That girl. Six hundred francs, if you're interested."

"Well, I'm not," I said. "I haven't got 600 francs and anyway she looks like somebody's mother."

"I know," he said. "But it's 600 francs even so."

He didn't explain how he knew and since I had to pay for his beer and he was wondering whether he could settle his hotel bill with a cheque I didn't like to enquire too deeply.

But it seemed an excessively high price to me at roughly 9p to the franc, even allowing for V.A.T. Certainly, if I can believe the newspapers I've been reading since my return, it's a good deal more than people have been paying for similar commodities in London.

Along with beer at 45p a glass and coffee at 20p a cup it's probably another ominous sign of how the cost of living will rise with membership of the E.E.C. But, of course, these things are open to negotiation, although it might be a wise precaution – whether in a bar, a café or a more secluded place – to haggle over the price before sampling the pleasures on offer.

One night a fearful rumpus broke out in a hotel along the Croisette, the participants being a man and a woman and the point at issue whether the sum involved was 150 or 200 francs, he inclining rather firmly toward the former and she insisting on the latter.

It would have been interesting, and no doubt instructive to anyone likely to find himself (or indeed herself) in a similar predicament, to know how the dispute was resolved. Unfortunately, the shouting stopped after the door of the adjoining room was flung open and a stout, red-faced and furious Englishman, clad only in a white towelling robe, hurtled into the corridor crying, "For pity's sake, give her the money and let me sleep."

I don't wish, you understand, to give the impression that Cannes at the time of the film festival is concerned only with such carnal matters. In truth it is actually possible, if you plan your day carefully, to see films as well.

But there is, as Mr Lindsay Anderson pointed out when, with righteous anger, he brushed aside a group of photographers who, instead of taking pictures of him – the director of the film that was about to open – were taking pictures of an unknown starlet on the steps of the cinema, an element of vulgarity about the place.

An English actor of my acquaintance who lives in France and normally likes the Carlton Hotel, headquarters of festival activities, always avoids it at this time of year on the grounds that its foyer corresponds exactly to his vision of hell, being eternally full of all the people he had hoped were dead already.

These are the people who go round congratulating each other on their films, saying, "George, what can I say? – you've done it again"; or, "Melvin, that was, gee, that was some remarkable picture"; or, "Fred, I just wish I hadn't been so tired when I saw your film."

Such remarks are skilfully worked out, since they can be taken as compliments (which they usually are, many film-makers being certifiable megalomaniacs) without actually being compliments.

Keen students of the language can also interpret them as meaning, "George, only you could have followed your last stinker with another stinker"; or, "Melvin, what the hell was it about?" or, "Fred, I was so bored I only woke up for the end credits."

Candour is reserved for conversations in which neither speaker has a vested interest in the film under review. For instance, "Did you see the movie last night?"

"Yeah. Terrible. People walked out."

"That's nothing. I've known people walk out of his movies on Jumbo jets and that ain't easy."

There is only one recorded instance of anyone giving an honest opinion to a film-maker and that was an English journalist who was so misguided as to tell a French producer that his picture was decadent and disgraceful and was summarily punished by having his dinner invitation withdrawn, a very grave matter at the Cannes Film Festival.

"See those two?" said the man on the terrace of the Carlton Hotel another night. "One thousand francs, the pair." He looked haggard and worn and asked if I'd like to buy his watch.

May 28, 1973

Dream Topping

I have to announce with deep regret the impending death of Walter Mitty, a lifelong companion of mine and, I daresay, of yours. The U.S. Navy has found a way to kill him – an anti-daydream machine that monitors concentration by measuring the brainwaves and sends out alarm signals when the victim's thoughts begin to wander.

The day of Big Brother is upon us, though I concede that such a contraption might have a legitimate application if wired to the likes of train drivers, pilots and the man with the finger on the H-bomb button.

It's not, perhaps, entirely desirable to have, say, an air-traffic control officer talking an aircraft in to land with half his mind while the other half meditates upon the treats to be found beneath the sweater of that blonde ground hostess, the one with the saucy eyes and no bra, brazen hussy, I don't know what girls are coming to these days, thank goodness, but I mean, going around with a pair like that and no bra, it's just not fair, somebody ought to tell her . . . hey, yeah, what if I give her my wolfish Robert Redford smile and say, "Don't you point those things at me, they might . . ." well, you know, something sharp and witty like that and then she'd say, "Oh, Cuthbert, at last! For months I've worshipped you from afar, well, all us girls have, so debonair, so dashing, so handsome, but I never in my wildest dreams imagined . . . oh, darling, quick – in my office, help me with these buttons, oh, Cuthbert, Cuthbert . . ."

Meanwhile, in the Concorde circling above the captain says, "Roger and out", or whatever, and pointing the aircraft vaguely downwards, returns to the eighteenth at St Andrews, saying to his gnarled and wizened caddy, "The moment of truth, McHaggis."

And McHaggis shakes his gnarled and wizened head and says, "Aye, sir, ye canna win the Open unless ye're doon in one frae here, shattering the course record by fifteen shots."

And the captain laughs his famous, reckless laugh, causing several women to swoon, and says, "Well, McHaggis, desperate situations need desperate remedies. Hand me my putter."

46

And McHaggis gives a gnarled and wizened gasp and says, "But, sir, it's nearly 400 yards. That's a bonny wee putt. Ye canna do it, sir!" And the captain says, "Can't I, McHaggis, can't I? Watch this . . ."

Whereupon he lands the Concorde in a cul-de-sac just off the Harrow Road.

In that situation a machine that goes "barp, barp" and "beep, beep" whenever Cuthbert or the captain allow their concentration to lapse could have its uses. But under normal circumstances – never.

Just imagine the bedlam in a Tube if such a machine went off whenever a trim and pretty secretary took her proper place in the blue movie being projected on the back of the eyeballs of the businessman sitting opposite, apparently engrossed in his newspaper.

Imagine, too, the scene at the forthcoming Commonwealth conference as our Ted rises to address his colleagues, saying, "Well, now, item twelve on the agenda – Rhodesia and all that stuff . . ." Were he wired for daydreams I have little doubt that his speech would go something like this . . .

"As I said to Ian Smith . . . Avast, ye lubbers! Furl the hatches, batten the mainbrace, splice the tops'ls!" Barp, barp, beep, beep. "Er, Ian I said, we'll give . . Cowes a race it'll never forget! What gaining on us, are they? We're lying too low in the water – throw out one of the crew!" Beep, beep, barp, barp. "Um, Ian, I said, ah, on the one hand or possibly on the other hand or, indeed, on all hands . . . on deck! Weigh the anchor! Shiver me timbers! No, lads, no, there's no need to carry me shoulder high through the length and breadth of the Isle of Wight while whistling 'All the nice girls love a sailor'. . . Beep, beep, beep . . ."

The next time I'm called in to the England team to replace Geoff Boycott, or step modestly on to the platform to receive my third Nobel Prize for Literature while the audience nudge one another and whisper, "See how unspoiled he is by his great success", I don't want a little box sending out such shrill notes of alarm that the girl across the bus says, "I don't know what you've got on your mind, buster, but the answer's definitely no."

July 30, 1973

Pick of the Weak

Naturally I rejoice along with the members of Women's Lib that the days of sex discrimination in industry are now officially over, even if one or two anomalies still remain.

It is, for instance, a clear case of male chauvinist piggery that women are not to be allowed to take their rightful place down the mines, although any girl who feels that her lifelong dream has been shattered by this restriction can console herself, as she lies sobbing into her pillow, with the thought that a shift at the coal-face, engaging and companionable work though it may be, can be absolute hell on one's manicure.

There is, after all, as every girl knows, more to life than swinging a pick-axe and no young miner would relish the thought of hurrying, freshly showered, from the pit-head to keep a date with that saucy young chit of a shorthand-typist she'd picked up on the bus, only to find him sulking behind his port and lemon in the saloon bar and complaining bitterly that unless she did something about her broken fingernails all bets were off because she'd laddered his nylon pants again last night.

In any case, the fact that women are banned from the mines gives Women's Lib something still to fight for. Under the new regulations they're in the happy position of having most of the cake and yet being able to clamour for the crumbs that are left – the equal right, for example, to be not only miners but also parsons and butlers and commanders of the armed forces: jobs that any girl would lust after.

However, there are certain aspects of this new equality that I do rather regret, especially the frowning upon advertisements for 'dolly bird" secretaries and "Girl Fridays", coming as it does just when someone has put forward the eminently sensible proposal that, after a hard day's slaving over a hot dictating-machine, man and secretary should go in for a spot of mutual massage.

No doubt such activities have not been unknown for some time between consenting adults, usually in the broom cupboard or that dark corner under the stairs. And no doubt, too, such innocent massage applied purely in the interests of soothing away the tensions of the daily grind, has frequently led to deeper, more significant and ultimately more satisfying relationships between numerous men and their Girl Fridays.

But since equality of opportunity is to cut both ways, will it be the same, I ask myself, if a man advertising for a secretary may no longer specify that he wants a dolly bird or a Girl Friday? Will he feel quite as enthusiastic about having his neck massaged by a dolly chap or a Boy Friday? I can't help suspecting that a lot of the fun is going to disappear from all this new-found office freedom if the secretary sitting on the boss's knee to take dictation weighs fifteen stone and plays in the pack for Rosslyn Park, although, of course, *chacun à son goût*.

What it boils down to, I suppose, is that in the days when I had a secretary (as opposed to the part-time services of my wife who, at the end of a day of lying to my creditors and all those people whom

I'd promised faithfully to phone last month, has no inclination at all to massage the back of my neck, save with a blunt instrument) I did like it to be a girl secretary.

A dolly-bird secretary for preference but a bird of some sort anyway. You can forgive a girl a lot that you couldn't possibly forgive a man. And frankly I'm not sure whether I could cope with this kind of 9 a.m. situation in the office:

"Oh, God, isn't the post done yet? Where's Arthur?"

"In the loo, having a bit of a cry."

"What, again? Not another broken love affair – who is it this time?"

"The sales manager. I warned him against her. I told him she was known to the boys in the typing pool as 'Interdeflora' but he wouldn't listen. She pinched his bottom in the lift and he was head over heels in love."

"Typical of Arthur, scatterbrained little fool. What happened?"

"Oh, she didn't turn up for a date last night and he found her in a compromising position with one of the office cleaners – the husky one with 'Mum' tattoed on his arm."

"Poor old Arthur. Perhaps I'd better take him out for a drink – cheer him up, you know."

"Ethel, keep your hands off Arthur. Good secretaries are hard to find."

September 24, 1973

Kuala Bare

When they get around to nominating the Man of the Year I hope someone puts in an urgent word on behalf of the chap in Kuala Lumpur who's just been arrested for seducing a hundred women in two years.

Read quickly, that may not sound like much. But pause awhile for reflection and the magnitude of the man's achievement is positively breathtaking. Allowing him a fortnight's annual holiday – and I should think he'd need at least that – it means he must have seduced a fresh (or anyway a different) woman *every week for two years*.

Well, I've known some pretty formidable operators in my time but this lad leaves them all, as it were, standing. His devotion to duty inspires nothing less than awe. Consider the fruitless, exhausting weeks most of us have spent trying to seduce just one woman; and then imagine the intolerable pressure of waking up every Monday morning in the knowledge that unless there's a new notch on your belt by next Saturday night your average is going to be shot to hell.

What I'd be most interested to learn, though, is his motive. Was he merely trying to establish a Malaysian All-Comers' Record? Or was he activitated by a sense of public service? Did he, as he sallied forth in search of each week's ration, murmur encouragingly to himself: "It's a dirty job, Charlie, but *somebody's* gotta do it"?

However, until I read about the hero of Kuala Lumpur my choice for Man of the Year would have been the bloke who once seduced the future Duchess of Bedford in a hotel in Manchester – a complete stranger, he was, who simply walked into her room, very tall and wearing a smile. For the next three days, apparently, that smile was all he did wear. "I tried to scream," says the Duchess in her memoirs, "but . . . the cry died in my throat. Not once did the smile leave his face . . . We stayed together for three days . . . I was introduced to a kind of sensuous animal loving that I did not know existed . . ."

Now what, do you suppose, prompted him – apart, of course, from the obvious fact that since it was Manchester it must have been raining and there wasn't a whole lot else to do? No play at Old Trafford, I dare say.

Still, never mind that. What worries me about the Duchess's story is the repercussions it's likely to have. In the time of which she writes there was no Women's Lib and any girl anxious for a similar kind of adventure could only wait in her room keeping her fingers crossed that the door might open and a tall, smiling stranger would come in, causing the cry to die in her throat.

But nowadays no girl of spirit is going to hang about waiting for tall, smiling strangers. Inspired by the Duchess's tale, she'll nip out and grab one and who can tell how many innocent commercial travellers are now going to vanish into the depths of Manchester hotels, never to be seen for three days? And how on earth are they going to explain to their wives?

"Ernie Postlethwaite, where . . . have . . . you . . . *been*?"

"Well, you'll never believe this, Gladys, but I was in my room at the hotel when the door opened and a tall, smiling stranger came in. Naturally, I tried to scream but the cry died in my throat, Gladys. Not once did the smile leave her face – at least I don't think it did. I didn't see a lot of her face, Gladys, for I was introduced to a kind of sensuous animal loving that I did not know existed . . ."

Well, never mind that either. The point is that while the Duchess's friend clearly deserves a mention in despatches, if not a citation for meritorious conduct, he has certainly been eclipsed in the contest for Man of the Year by the Herculean events in the Far East. After all, while one future duchess in three days is a highly respectable score by any standards, what the judges will wish to know is: what did he do for the other 49½ working weeks of the year?

April 1, 1974

51

Goodness knows what life must have been like in France at the weekend if the strike went ahead as planned. It was called, as you may have read, by Women's Lib which, in the cause of equality and freedom, urged all wives, mistresses, and girl-friends to stop work and refuse to make love.

Not a particularly original ploy, of course. Lysistrata and her mates were at it, with varing degrees of success, as far back as 411 B.C. But on the face of things, France would seem to be the ideal country for women to pull this particular caper since legend has it that all Frenchmen are extraordinarily randy fellows who, in spite of the handicap of smelling constantly of garlic and caporal tobacco, are gifted and enthusiastic operators forever on the *qui vive*.

Frankly, I've never been entirely sure how much credence to lend to this image. I suspect that it's been cunningly manufactured over the years by the French tourist office to persuade impressionable and potentially naughty girls to spend their holiday money on the Côte d'Azur rather than, say, the Costa Brava, where the most exciting thing that's likely to happen to them is that they get goosed by a Spanish waiter.

Indeed, my own observation of the average Frenchman is that he's a surly and ill-mannered character, not especially personable and, on balance, somewhat more interested in *boules* than *poules*.

But if we give the legend the benefit of the doubt and also assume that the strike was carried out efficiently then France must have been a frightful place this weekend, the air being full of the stern, feminine sound of *"Non, Henri, absolument non"* and the answering cries, moans, entreaties and general gibbering of desperate Frenchmen deprived of their oats.

However, quite apart from the suggestion implicit in the strike that making love is a pastime enjoyed only by men and regarded by women as simply another household chore to be fitted in somewhere between washing up the supper things and making the bedtime cocoa, another thought occurs to me, namely: would such a strike be effective here?

I must say I have my doubts. As a matter of fact I'm pretty sure it would pass unnoticed. The reputation of the Frenchman may, or may not, be deserved but that of the Briton as a man who abandons love-making as soon as he discovers what is causing all those children certainly is.

It's his attitude, surely, that causes the British girl abroad to be regarded as game akin to the partridge which, when pursued, flutters a few yards and then flops down in abject surrender. Thus the British housewife who marched into the sitting-room one Friday night and said, "Fred, I have an important announcement to make – as from now I'm on strike till Monday morning", would most probably be answered with an anguished cry of, "Move over, can't you? Your father wasn't a glazier you know."

"Pardon?"

"You're in front of the telly and I'm watching the action replay of the Bugner fight, though how they have the nerve to call it *action* I don't know! Action? Clobber him, Joe, Clobber the fat Wop! Gawd, he's hopeless – couldn't hit a cow on the ass with a shovel."

"Did you hear me, Fred? I'm on strike – no more cooking, no more housework."

"What? Oh, yeah, all right. Look, don't worry, I'll get something down the boozer, chicken-in-the-basket or something. I'll be okay."

"Listen, I don't think you understand. I'm on a total strike – I'm not going to make love till Monday at the earliest."

"Well, I should certainly hope not, Ethel! You're a married woman, after all. Making love? The very idea! Who's been chatting you up – that bloody milkman, I'll bet . . ."

No, it seems to me that a Lysistrata strike in Britain would be quite hopeless. And, to be fair, I doubt if it would be any more effective if, should the necessity arise, the tactic were adopted by British men. They would certainly be relieved to know that they were forbidden by their unions to fulfil their conjugal rights throughout the weekend or more, but if they arrived home and said, "Ethel, I'm on strike. I'm not making love till Monday", their wives would probably look up from their knitting and murmuring "Purl one, plain one", would say, "Oh, yes? What else is new?"

It's a question of horses for courses, really. A no-equality, no-sex strike might cause dismay in France but over here it would most likely be celebrated as a national holiday.

June 3, 1974

Robing Red Breasts

The debate that appears to be dividing the whole of France at the moment – the French having this happy knack of getting their priorities right – is over the question of topless sunbathing.

According to a poll conducted by *France-Soir*, 51 per cent of the population is opposed to it while 49 per cent is in favour, the minority being composed mainly of Parisians (a notoriously licentious lot), Socialists (ditto) and wealthy men, (ditto, ditto and then some); the most ardent, even indeed hysterical proponent of topless sunbathing being, presumably, a Socialist millionaire with a flat on the Champs-Élysées. A kind of Gallic Harold Lever perhaps, although on more mature consideration I'm not at all convinced.

Those opposed to this essentially harmless and to the practitioner, as well as the onlooker, possibly beneficial pastime consist largely of women (notorious spoilsports), workers (ditto) and small farmers. I'm a bit confused about the small farmers since it's unclear whether the reference is to men who run small farms or small men who happen to be farmers.

It's understandable that farmers, *per se*, might adopt a conservative attitude in the matter since a topless sunbather, reclining in a field, could easily distract the attention of a haymaker, thus causing him to do himself irreparable harm with the pitchfork.

But why small farmers as opposed to large ones? Unless, of course, it's felt that a farmer built on the lines of de Gaulle could stroll across a whole beach full of blush-pink bosoms, slowly ripening in the sun, and by keeping his gaze level and his mind on higher things not be offended by the sight; while a farmer of more Napoleonic stature would have to keep his mind level and his gaze on higher things if his eye were not be assaulted by the reproachful, unblinking stare of a regiment of toasting nipples.

However, the entire problem, as is so often the way in France, is academic. In theory the penalty for over-exposure likely to cause distress to women, workers and small farmers – though not to Parisians, Socialists and wealthy men – is a fine of £100.

But in practice, and to my personal knowledge, the flics have been keeping a bulging eye on the situation throughout the length and breadth of the Riviera for at least three years now and don't appear to have caught anybody yet. It's not, I think, that in fact nobody actually sunbathes topless on the Riviera but that the police make such an elephantine row as they come whooping and trumpeting hoarsely across the sands that the most sun-dazed sunbather has ample time to pull on her bikini top before the custodians of the law arrive, saying sternly: "I've caught you red-breast . . . er, hand . . . er, your over arrest, I mean under-exposed . . . No, dammit, let me start again . . ."

Interestingly, though, the *France-Soir* poll also reveals that 56 per cent of those interviewed were – after what is described as an "impassioned" debate – opposed to total nudity on the beaches. In this I believe they are right, for as it happens I can cite a cautionary tale that underlines the dangers of nude bathing.

Some friends of mine once motored down to the South Coast to dine with friends of theirs who had rented a seaside cottage right on the beach. When they arrived they found only their host to greet them, his wife being in bed and indisposed.

As the evening wore on he explained what had happened. That afternoon he had gone swimming while his wife remained in the cottage preparing the dinner. This done, she had walked on to the beach and there seen her husband, fresh from the sea and totally nude, bending down towards her to pull on his underpants.

She had, therefore, as any wife might, crept up behind him and assaulted him jovially but rather vulgarly, crying the while: "Ding dong". The man had then leapt up startled, as any man might, and spinning round quickly had revealed that far from being her husband he was, in fact, a total stranger.

The wife had uttered a scream of horror and gone into a fit of the vapours from which she failed to emerge for several days. Had *France-Soir* been able to put that story about while they canvassed the populace they might have found that even Parisian Socialist millionaires would have marked an unhesitating *"Non"* against nude bathing.

July 15, 1974

Fun and Games

The conference at Bradford University on psycho-sexual problems was a considerable eye-opener to me. I followed the reports with keen interest and I'm bound to say, having led a somewhat sheltered life, that I'd never realised sex was quite such a complicated business.

For instance, it was with a good deal of open-mouthed horror that I read of the existence of the Brunnhilde-type woman who, according to Dr Prudence Tunnadine of the Family Planning Association, says that a man must be strong enough to overcome her in battle before he can have her.

Well, all right, I've heard of one chap fighting another chap for a lady's favours. But, intent to rape apart, the prospect of actually squaring up to the lady herself is something that had never occurred to me.

I mean, I don't honestly know how long my enthusiasm could last if the warm-up to the main event took the form of a full display of the martial arts, with the light of my life dancing round the bedroom shouting "Float like a butterfly, sting like a bee" while administering the full range of karate chops to the throat, half-nelsons, cross-buttocks, thumbs-in-the-eye, knees-in-the-groin, two pinfalls, a knock-out or a submission to decide the winner and bringing the whole affair to a conclusion with a perfect hook-off-the-jab.

The thing about the Brunnhilde-type woman, said Dr Tunnadine, is "not that she fights, which is exciting, but that she wins, which is disappointing". Well, yes, I'd say that was disappointing. I'd say that any man who approached his spouse with love in his heart only to find himself, a few minutes later, lying stunned on the floor, bleeding from the nose and mouth and with his left eye closed while she stood over him sucking her knuckles and proclaiming, "I am the greatest, I am the prettiest", would be entitled, at the very least, to feel the odd pang of disappointment.

The other aspect of the Bradford conference which engaged my attention was the claim by Dr Thomas Main, medical director of a Surrey hospital, that if a man afflicted with impotency can overcome that problem, his whole life becomes more potent.

"He gets a better job, more money, a better house and so on," said Dr Main. "He enjoys life as a whole." One imagines this happy fellow leaping light-footed up the executive ladder, moving from maisonette to semi to country mansion, his wallet bulging, an object of envy and admiration to all who know him and murmuring to himself, in the manner of the newspaper advertisements, "Thinks – thanks to sex!"

As a specific example, however, Dr Main cited a soccer player who went from the reserves into the first team as soon as he'd sorted out his love problems. This equating of sex with soccer is an entirely new concept to me but, on reflection, I suppose it does stand up to examination.

Here, for example, is a hypothetical analysis of the soccer player under review: "He used to be a real goer, a ninety-minute performer – but now he's lost his stamina, his work rate's fallen off, his distribution is terrible, he's weak on the flanks, hopeless in midfield, can't do a thing right in the penalty area and he hasn't scored in weeks."

The point is, who do you suppose would be speaking – his manager or his wife? Tricky, isn't it? But, on the other hand, I imagine that if he were able to sort out those matters in one field of endeavour everything would click into place in the other as well.

The problem, I daresay, was that the atmosphere wasn't right at home because of the absence of a crowd. Most footballers say it's difficult to raise your game in the Stiffs because there's nobody to cheer you on. So what Dr Main's soccer player probably did was to create big-match tension by persuading the neighbours to stand in the garden rhythmically chanting his name, waving rattles and throwing toilet rolls through the bedroom window. With such encouragement he'd have hit mid-season form both at home and on the field in no time at all.

Fascinating, and no doubt of great interest to footballers everywhere. But what struck me about that Bradford conference was the sacrilegious thought that perhaps the modern preoccupation with sex had gone just a little too far. Everyone talks a good fight these days but if they'd just stop chatting and get on with it, as and when the fancy took them, there'd surely be far fewer problems and hardly any need at all for conferences.

September 16, 1974

Who Goes Home?

Mr Charles Irving, who is both a bachelor and the Conservative Member for Cheltenham, says that many M.P.s are sex-starved and ought to have a trade union.

The link between these two statements, delivered in more or less the same breath, strikes me as a little tenuous, unless of course Mr Irving, being a Tory and therefore presumably not a trades unionist, has somehow conceived the notion that unions are now so far committed to providing for the creature comforts of their members, that miners and dockers and the like hold their branch meetings in the back parlour of the local bordello, while wallowing in the warm embraces of Miss Whiplash and French Model, 19.

But assuming that he is correct in his first assertion, namely that because of "the obscene hours" they work many M.P.s are sex-starved, the point that puzzles me is: how on earth does he know? I have, in my time, worked in a number of offices for a variety of organisations and I think I can honestly say that, without exception, the state of their carnal cravings and deprivations is something which my colleagues have very decently kept to themselves. It's not, I mean to say, a topic that is dropped lightly into the social badinage of the day or brought up at committee meetings under the heading of any other business.

But it may be, I suppose, that M.P.s are different, although I beg leave to doubt it. Are we, after all, to assume that when Mr Irving clocks in at the House and encounters the leader of his party the following conversation is likely to take place: "Good morning, Mrs T. and how are you today?"

"Oh, not too bad at all, thank you, Charles. Bit sex-starved, you know."

"Ah, welcome to the club, Mrs T. I'm frightfully randy myself."

Surely not. Nor is it very likely that when, say, Mr Wilson and Mr Benn are to be seen in earnest conference what they're actually saying is . . .

"Ayoop, Wedgie lad, tha looks a mite sex-starved this morning."

"Oh, thank you, Prime Minister. Of course what I'm really aiming for is a sort of lean, hungry, intellectually passionate look. I suck in my cheeks and frown a lot, you know. It goes down awfully well with the left-wingers– makes them remember how concerned I am and forget how very rich I am."

"Aye, well, like I said, lad, tha's looking more sex-starved than intellectually passionate but happen t'left-wingers won't know t'difference."

Mr Irving doesn't say whether he, personally, is sex-starved and it would be indelicate of me to speculate upon the matter, especially as I don't know the man. Neither does he give any clue as to whether his remarks are the result of idle speculation, an informed guess based upon observation of conduct, or a scientific investigation carried out perhaps by means of an opinion poll of his fellow members asking, "How sex-starved are you – not at all/slightly/never think about it/long past it/very/to the exclusion of all else? Strike out whichever is inapplicable."

However, the same paper that reported his complaint also went about canvassing the views of M.P.s' wives, and Mrs Lisanne Radice, wife of the Labour Member for Chester-le-Street and leader of the Campaign for Effective Parliamentary Hours, said, "These really late night sittings mean that M.P.s can't be so effective the next morning when they have to make crucial decisions."

Well, I feel it would be improper of us to spend too much time contemplating the ineffectiveness of M.P.s the next morning or the nature of the crucial decisions they may be called upon to make, although by all means feel free to do so if you wish. What we ought to think about instead is what happens when they get to the Commons and find they aren't so effective and have to make crucial decisions.

Are they to be found, as Mr Irving would seem to suggest, prowling the corridors of the House with their loins on fire and their minds occupied less with the ramifications of the capital-transfer tax or the plight of Norton-Villiers-Triumph than with the setting up of a Select Committee to investigate the possibility of installing relief-massage parlours and a hot line to the business premises of the nearest Italian teacher (38–24–38)?

Possibly they are. And possibly all that astonishing shouting and fighting that goes on in the Chamber isn't caused by a clash of political ideologies at all but by sheer physical frustration.

March 10, 1975

Skirting the Issue

I hadn't realised until Mr Ronald Bell pointed it out in the House the other day that there was a lavatory clause in the Sex Discrimination Bill but I must say that I'm very relieved to hear it.

As a matter of fact I'd been worrying about this for some time, though naturally I had not wished to bring it up for reasons of delicacy. But the thought had occurred that if doors which had hitherto been clearly – though discriminatingly – marked "Ladies" and "Gentlemen" or "Men" and "Women" were in future to bear the uninformative legend "Persons", a certain amount of confusion might ensue.

What on earth would one do, for instance, if in a moment of extreme urgency on Waterloo Station one were to burst thankfully through a door that said "Persons" only to find the place full of . . .

well, I don't wish to use offensive and sexual discriminatory words like "women" but, let us say, persons who were not quite the same sort of persons as oneself?

I mean, there one would be hopping about with one's legs crossed and in no mood for idle chatter and there they would be squeaking indignantly, "Get out of here! Can't you see this is a 'Persons'? What are you – some kind of dirty old person?"

"Madam," one would say . . . no, no, sorry – scrub that. Not "madam", of course. Start using filthy talk like that and before you knew where you were you'd be up before the Sexual Relations Board on a grave charge of premeditated male chauvinism.

"Person," one would say, with as much dignity as one could muster in the circumstances, "I am fully aware that this is a 'Persons'. It says so clearly on the door and since I am undoubtedly a person myself (and could indeed prove it by showing you the entry in my passport where it states 'Sex: person') I have every intention of using it. Furthermore, if you don't permit me to enter the first vacant cubicle immediately I shall be unable to answer for the consequences."

Whereupon, presumably, one would dive urgently through the crowd and avail oneself of the facilities, while the spokesperson of the protesting group said, "Ethel, call a policeperson at once."

But even that could lead to further complications because very likely Ethel would get as far as the door before pausing, doubtfully, and saying, "Er, what kind of policeperson, Gladys?"

"What kind? A uniformed policeperson, of course."

"Yes, but . . ." And here she would lower her voice apologetically . . . "Do forgive me, Gladys, and I promise not to use the word again but you do mean a 'lady' policeperson, I suppose?"

"My God!" Gladys would say, smiting herself on the brow with the heel of her hand, "has the fight against sexual discrimination been entirely in vain? Can I believe the evidence of my ears? Did I truly hear one of our own number lapsing into the archaic and dishonoured language of male chauvinism? There are no 'ladies' any more, Ethel. There are no 'gentlemen' either, nor 'men' nor 'women'. There are only persons."

"Yes, I know, Gladys. But . . ."

"Oh, use your loaf, Ethel. Go find a policeperson in a skirt."

Exit a shamefaced Ethel to seek out a beskirted policeperson and inform same that a perverted old person had invaded the "Persons" and refused to leave. The policeperson would then charge through the nearest door marked "Persons", blowing her whistle, and discover the horrifying sight of a whole row of obvious dirty old persons standing side by side in porcelain stalls and staring meditatively at the wall.

"All right, you perverted lot," she would say. "You're under arrest."

This would certainly have the effect of startling the assembled company out of their respective reveries, causing them to look sharply over their shoulders to the serious detriment of their footwear.

"Get out of here!" they would say. "Can't you see this is a 'Persons'?" And in their outrage they would spin round angrily to face the intruder and be immediately arrested for indecent exposure.

Well, no doubt while all this was being sorted out the original interloper in the "Persons" next door would have had time to complete his business and make good his escape. But the basic problem would have remained unsolved. Just as well then that our legislature was farsighted enough to foresee such difficulties and to ensure, presumably, that although men and women are undoubtedly equal in all else, in matters of public convenience it's still a question of *vive la difference*. Had it been otherwise we should soon be needing a Lavatory Discrimination Bill that included a sexual clause.

March 31, 1975

2

Of Atastroke and Harold, Old Mother Hubbard and Wedgie and other political animals

The Loss of the Moonstone

The story so far: After wandering in the political wilderness, the Mighty Atastroke emerges at the festival of the general election where he finds that the people are gullible. "Put your faith in me," he says, "and the quality of life shall be good and the rise in the cost of living shall cease." Then, chanting the magic word "Atastroke!" he turns himself into a near facsimile of a prime minister. Now read on . . .

The months went by and it was as the Mighty Atastroke had promised. The quality of life improved so much that 929,000 people were no longer called upon to go to work. Some, too foolish to value this gift of unlimited leisure, were ungrateful and tried to find jobs; but Atastroke and his minions turned them away with firm but kindly words. "Stand on your own two feet" they said. And many tried to do so and fell down and were much confused, particularly those on the Upper Clyde.

And there was yet more confusion when the cost of living was seen not only to rise but to soar; and the people were dismayed and asked "Why does not the Mighty Atastroke do as he vowed?" Then another minion, the Minister for Cows and Crops, soothed them saying, "Surely nobody took that stuff seriously", and the people understood. It was simply Atastroke's little jest. Goodness, how the people laughed. And how the Mighty Atastroke laughed and how his shoulders heaved and his teeth shone to think how well his jest had worked and how he had fooled most of the people for much of the time. And so, when the International Monetary Fund revealed that consumer prices in Britain had risen by a wondrous 10·3 per cent within a year, the people were philosophical and said, "Strange are the ways of Atastroke." And they tightened their belts.

But the Mighty One turned away their wrath, saying that the ills of the past year had been the work of his evil predecessor who had laid such curses upon the land as too much taxation and wasteful Government spending and high wages that led to unemployment. And he summoned his senior minions to meet him at the mansion called Chequers, where these curses would be lifted and eyes would be kept on the way ahead. Yet he seemed to have lost faith in the magic word for he spoke it not. But the people remembered. And those for whom the quality of life was good and for whom money and work presented no problem, since they had little or none of either, dreamt of the next festival of the general election when they might themselves cry "Atastroke!" and send him back whence he had come.

Next: What else has the Mighty Atastroke in store for Britain? And how high can prices go? And how many more people need never go to work again? Watch the meeting at Chequers on Friday

week and the Conservative Party conference for further thrilling instalments.

Guardian Leader Column
September 27, 1971

The Rosy Brush of Dawn

Did you see that picture of gallant Mrs Patrick Jenkin doing her bit to save power? God, it was moving. Do you know what she's done, plucky little woman – she's actually taken to doing the washing-up herself *by hand*!

I can hear the astonished gasps reverberating round the land. "Not . . . Good Lord! . . . You don't mean . . .?" But yes, I do. Not for Mrs Patrick Jenkin, wife of Mr Patrick Jenkin of the Department of Energy, not for her the electricity-consuming automatic dishwasher, nor even the apple-cheeked char scraping bacon fat off the plates – just Mrs Jenkin and the Fairy Liquid tackling the job together. What's more she's turned her fridge off, too. I still get this sort of choked-up feeling every time I think of it.

What a family they are, those Jenkins, what an example they set. It was people like that who built the Empire, you know. I mean, just picture them at home – downstairs, in the kitchen, Mrs Jenkin washing up with her very own hands and upstairs, in the bathroom, Mr Jenkin cleaning his teeth in the dark.

I bet you, now lavatory paper's in short supply, that if you crept into their bathroom while Mr Jenkin was cleaning his teeth and shone a torch you'd see old pages of *Hansard* hanging up on a bit of string beside the loo.

Of course, we can't all hope to emulate the Jenkins. For a start he's obviously one of those efficient men who knows at any given moment where to lay his hands on his teeth.

You won't catch him in the early morning groping his way to the head of the stairs, tripping over the dog, stubbing his toe on the cat and shouting in a loud mumble over the sound of shattering crockery as once again, in the pitch-black kitchen, brave Mrs Jenkin misses the sink and hurls another stack of plates out of the window, "Darling, have you seen my teeth?"

Nor will there then ensue one of those exasperating, fruitless exchanges that take place in less-organised households. "No, I've not seen your teeth. Where did you have them last?"

"I can't remember. I didn't leave them in that restaurant, did I?"

"Don't think so. Did you look under the bed? Or in the ashtray? Hold on, though. I think the dog's got 'em. He's burying something out there in the garden . . ."

No; Mr Jenkin could find his teeth all right, even assuming they're not growing healthily in his mouth, no matter how dark it was. Just there, they are, in that tumbler beside the bedside reading candle, set permanently in the modest yet defiant and slightly mocking smile of the crisis beater.

Let us then imagine the early morning scene *chez* Jenkin. It is the hour before dawn and Mr Jenkin, rising like the lark, teeth in hand, ventures on to the unlit landing, pulls open a door and plunges confidently into the airing cupboard. Undeterred he starts again and by a process of trial and error comes triumphantly to the bathroom.

And then – what? Does he fumble about trying to plug in his electric toothbrush? I doubt it. His electric razor is already occupying the socket and besides I daresay he cleans his teeth with an ordinary hand-powered toothbrush. That done, still without benefit of light, he shaves (accidentally removing one eyebrow), dresses and falls downstairs having inadvertently put his trousers on back to front in the dark.

"What", he says, picking himself up with a light laugh, "is that curious smell?"

"Oh nothing, dear," says Mrs Jenkin. "Just the food rotting in the refrigerator. I turned it off, you know, to save power."

Mr Jenkin claps her on the back. (These crisis beaters are not men to show much emotion.) "Good old chap," he says gruffly. Thereupon he feels his way to the breakfast table, pours himself cereal from a packet and, taking barely fifteen minutes to locate the front door, goes off to work. It's only later, when dawn has broken, that Mrs Jenkin discovers he has not only eaten all the dog's biscuits but is still trying to find his way out of the downstairs cloakroom.

Never mind. There, I fancy, is a model for us all, an example of how to save resources that is quite perfect save perhaps in one small respect. There is, as you know, a water shortage in this country. Could not Mr Jenkin then blaze the trail in water-saving, too, by putting his teeth in with the washing-up?

January 21, 1974

Soap Opera

I'm sure you would all like to join with me in applauding those upright Tory M.P.s Mr John Stokes and Mr Joseph Kinsey for their condemnation of the grossly permissive Mrs Ida Jones.

As you may recall Mrs Jones won a £10 prize from the South-Eastern Gas Board for her advertising slogan: "Put a bit of romance into your bath by sharing the water."

Well, immediately Mr Stokes and Mr Kinsey spoke for all

decent-minded people everywhere by saying, respectively, "I think it's in the worst possible taste", and "I am deeply shocked."

Now before we go any further and while you are still wondering how a man with a name like Kinsey gets to be shocked at the idea of people taking a bath together, I think we must investigate just what it is that shocks. I believe it's this brazen assertion that romance might be introduced into the bath water. A bath, as Mr Stokes and Mr Kinsey would be quick to point out, is not for romantic dalliance.

A bath is for filling with ice-cold water, after a brisk early-morning run, and plunging into armed with a coarse-fibred loofah with which to flagellate one's limbs and dispel all unhealthy thoughts.

That being so, what – Mr Stokes and Mr Kinsey might ask – is likely to happen if Mrs Jones's licentious idea catches on and married couples leap into the bath together?

(We must, of course, assume that Mrs Jones intended her suggestion only for married couples. The mere thought that she might, light-heartedly, have aimed it at unmarried couples too would cause both Mr Stokes and Mr Kinsey to plunge into their second ice-cold bath of the day.)

Well, I'll tell you what would happen. In the first place, the bath would be so crowded that there'd be no room for Mr Stokes's rubber duck or Mr Kinsey's plastic yacht. And in the second place, unless they bathed in the dark (as Mr Patrick Jenkin surely does) men and women would be exposing themselves to each other *all bare*! Indeed, unless they averted their gaze they'd be in grave danger of catching a glimpse of each other's nasty, horrid Things.

From that point there's no end to the depravity that could break out. A couple so abandoned and crazed with lust as to bath together could easily throw all sense of propriety to the winds and actually proceed to sleep together in the same bed.

Furthermore, you know and I know and Mr Stokes and Mr Kinsey know, because they have it on quite reliable authority, that if married couples sleep together in the same bed utterly beastly events can take place, and, if they're extremely unlucky, babies can occur.

Worse still, if they become so addicted to the vile practice of bathing and sleeping together that they pursue it for a number of years, several babies could occur before they find out what's been causing it. At that point, one hopes, they would come belatedly to their senses, overwhelmed with revulsion and disgust at their own lewdness, and make every effort to kick their pernicious habits.

Ideally, they should withdraw at once to a convent or monastery there to spend their lives in penance, meditation and hair shirts, with framed and autographed portraits of Mr Stokes and Mr Kinsey hanging over their freezing, lonely baths to lend strength and inspiration when their spirit flags.

Inevitably, such a course may not be open to everybody as Mr Stokes and Mr Kinsey are tolerant and broad-minded enough to concede. In that case, the culprits should revert to the normal practice of clean-living people and take to sleeping in separate bedrooms with the doors and windows securely locked and bolted against temptation and each other.

As for bathing, well, the sensible course would be to give it up entirely. But if that proves impracticable then a rota system would have to be drawn up and, if possible, each partner should swear to leave the house while the other took a bath, otherwise and before you knew it they'd be saying, "Ah, come on. We've broken the habit now. One little bath together won't hurt us. Let's just try it to prove how strong we can be." And then it would be too late and they'd be back, this time perhaps irrevocably, in their furtive, twilight world of lubricity.

February 4, 1974

Leap Fog

"Good morning, Prime Minister."

"Ah' 'morning. What's that you've got there – lavatory paper? Managed to find some then? Well done, well done. We're running perilously short of order papers upstairs, I can tell you."

"Er, well, it's not actually lavatory paper, sir. It's the page proof for our pre-election advertisement in the newspapers."

"Never mind, it'll serve just as well. Hand it over. Might as well cast my eye through it, see if I can understand the jokes . . . I say! Who are these scruffy-looking herberts in the photograph?"

"Ah, yes, well they represent a pair of working-class chappies, sir."

"Do they, really? Good God, so that's what they look like, is it? I had no idea! Many of them about, are there?"

"Quite a few I believe, sir."

"Is that so? Well, well. Are they all like that, do you suppose – all peaky and ill-fed and wearing those frightful off-the-peg clothes? And, great Scott, look here – one of them's even wearing a sort of dreadful beret thing with a pom-pom on top. What can their tailors be thinking of to send them out like that?"

"Well, sir . . ."

"What a fearful pair of bounders. Oh, I say, that's rather good – bounders. They're playing leapfrog, you see. And, as a matter of interest, *why* are they playing leapfrog in the middle of the road like that? Have they no yachts to go to?"

"Yes, well, that's our slogan, sir – 'Leapfrog to disaster'. . ."

"Mind you, I like a game of leapfrog myself. Tones you up no

70

end, although of course it can lead to disaster. Good idea to warn the working-class chappies like that. I remember once on *Morning Cloud*, we were playing leapfrog, someone gave me a shove, I went right over the side – splash! Chaps playing a joke on me, naturally. I said, 'Quick, throw me a lifesaver.' They said they hadn't any lifesavers, would a Polo mint do instead? Great sense of humour, those fellows. Kept the joke up right to the end. They wouldn't pull me aboard, you know. I had to swim three miles to the nearest port."

"Yes, sir, very droll. Would you have a look at the text here, the bit about standing firm on pay and prices? 'That's the way to be fair', it says."

"Well, nothing wrong with that, is there? Nobody could be fairer than me, surely."

"Oh, no sir, certainly not. But there are moaners who claim it's not entirely fair that copy-typists at N.C.B. headquarters earn more than the miners."

"So they should. I mean, look at it this way – if you had a smart London office who would you want to do your copy-typing, pretty dolly birds or a bunch of sweaty great miners coughing their lungs up all over the place?"

"Well, since you put it like that . . ."

"No other way to put it. It's skilled work, copy-typing. Miners can't do it. They'd leave filthy thumbprints all over the paper. Anyway, there's the question of supply and demand. If you want girls to do your copy-typing you've jolly well got to pay them the wages they ask. Simple matter of economics."

"Of course! I hadn't seen it in that light, sir."

"Besides, I don't like miners. There's something very furtive about people who burrow away underneath the ground all day. It's not natural, you know. And have you seen the conditions they work in? Filthy! Can't have any truck with chaps like that."

"Yes, sir. Well, I'll just take these page proofs and . . ."

"Hold on. What's this at the bottom: 'Conservatives for ALL the people'? No, no, that's wrong. Better just add a bit to that – 'Conservatives for ALL the people, except miners. And Communists. And people who vote Labour or Liberal. And working-class chappies like these.' They really are genuine working-class chappies, are they?"

"I believe so, sir, although it's rumoured that they're actually a pair of small businessmen who went bankrupt as a result of your economic policies."

"Well, it amounts to the same thing, I daresay. They're working-class chappies now, whatever they were in the past. And if they carry on playing leapfrog in the streets in those shabby clothes they always will be. What they want to do is pop along to Savile Row, get a couple of decent suits and find themselves jobs with a smart property speculator. That's the only way to get on in this world."

February 11, 1974

Relative Value

What Britain was looking for, apparently, during the general election was not so much a prime minister as a mother. An article in *New Society* says so and it must be true because *New Society* knows about these things.

I won't go into the details of how it reached this conclusion but it seems the entire election campaign was riddled with clues that left no room for doubt in the mind of an experienced reader of entrails. I think it had to do with the way Harold favoured cosy words like "family" and "people" and Ted ranted on about "firmness" and "strength". Somehow this meant Britain sought a firm, strong mother who wanted all the people to be her family.

Put it this way: it's as if we, the nation, had collectively cast ourselves as Captain Hook sidling furtively up to Atastroke's Wendy and mumbling: "Will you be my mother?"; a thought that's not perhaps as preposterous as it first appears if you add another image of Lord Carrington as Peter Pan, leader of the Lost Boys, and Tony Barber flitting about like Tinker Bell.

In the event, of course, we changed our minds and rather messed up the scenario. When we were asked if we believed in fairies we all shouted "No!" and Tinker Bell's light went out; Peter was left consoling an hysterical Wendy and the electorate, having turned itself into a whole legion of Lost Boys, fled *en masse* from Never-Never Land and hurled itself into the arms of Mrs Darling, as portrayed by Harold Wilson.

And yet I don't know. In spite of what *New Society* says I have my doubts about the entire premise. I can't really see either Ted or Harold as my mother, although, in a curious way, I can envisage Jeremy Thorpe aspiring briefly to the role of Nana, a kind of surrogate mother, but being obliged to play Mr Darling, banished yet again to the kennel.

What spoils the original theory, possibly, is the fact that I don't believe Ted wanted to be Wendy in the first place. He wanted to be Captain Hook and make everybody walk the plank. "It's my ship," he kept shouting, "and if I can't be skipper you can all jolly well get off." So we did.

Anyway, Harold saw himself in a more swashbuckling role, too – not a mother but a halfback. His Government colleagues, he said on becoming Prime Minister, were the forwards and he was the halfback pushing the ball through to them – and a funny old team

73

that is, to be sure: about 97 forwards and one short, stout halfback providing all the passes.

A stirring analogy, I do agree, but alarmingly archaic nevertheless. There aren't any halfbacks any more. There hasn't been a halfback since Danny Blanchflower retired. You go up to Norman Hunter and call him a halfback and see what happens. He'll bite your leg off.

No, the halfbacks are called mid-field players these days and what kind of mid-field player is Harold going to be – a ball-carrier or a ball-winner? Is he going to feed the strikers or stop them? I suppose there was a straw in the wind last week when he did stop one lot of strikers, even though he felt it necessary to concede a penalty in the process.

Still, the game's in its early stages yet and if some may be a little appalled at the drastic result of Harold's two-footed sliding tackle I've no doubt he's already dismissed it airily as a professional foul and therefore quite justified, especially if it converts the national team from a bunch of part-timers into a squad of ninety-minute players.

Be that as it may, however, we can now see that the general election didn't actually provide us with a mother at all. It gave us instead this old-fashioned halfback distributing the ball from Lord North Street. ("Nay, Mary, leave t'plaster ducks on t'wall. I'm refusin' t'transfer to Downing Street.")

Furthermore, it also left us with the pitiful sight of an old sea dog not only stripped of his command through inadvertently running the ship on to the rocks, but deprived of his berth as well and forced to roam the streets of London homeless. ("Move along, sir, do. You know you can't sleep there. I don't care who you are, you'll find Rowton House a sight more comfortable than the Embankment, this weather.")

Nevertheless, I should like to think that *New Society* was on the right lines. How nice it would be to play Happy Families after three and a half years of Beggar Your Neighbour.

March 11, 1974

In a Flat Spinola

I always had this naïve conviction that the men who rule countries were somehow different from other people – men of *gravitas* and wisdom who had everything under control.

They'd always know where to lay their hands on a clean pair of socks. *They'd* never discover, as the inspector stood over them in a posture of cynical disbelief that they'd left their season ticket in their other suit. Rogues, villains and crooks they may be, I would say comfortingly to myself, but at least they're efficient rogues, villains and crooks.

But suddenly the scales have fallen from my eyes and my delusions lie choking in the dust, for the events of the past week have disclosed that the world's rulers run their countries much as I run my life – reeling, that is to say, from one unscheduled disaster to another.

The revelations from the White House, of course, come instantly to mind and are bloodcurdling enough even if you ignore the incidental information that President Nixon and his mates seem to spend their time sitting around his office effing and blinding at each other, and making casual plans to screw whichever member of the company doesn't happen to be in the room at the time.

But perhaps the finest example of the principle of government by monumental foul-up occurred during the coup in Portugal. When all plans had been laid and the hour to strike was at hand Dr Feytor Pinto, the intermediary, hurried from the presence of Dr Caetano with a rather important message of surrender for General Spinola only to discover as he hit the streets that he had no idea where the man lived.

What precisely happened next is not clear, but no doubt he returned to the Prime Minister's office and, clearing his throat sheepishly, said, "I say, you don't happen to know his address, do you?" At which point, I dare say, Dr Caetano said, "Turn the telly down, chaps, this is serious. Anyone know where Spinola lives?"

Much head-scratching among the conspirators. "Spinola? Spinola? Isn't he in the telephone book?" Naturally he wasn't. Anyone you want urgently is never in the telephone book. Dr Caetano, therefore, would have got on to Directory Inquiries and Directory Inquiries would have told him with ill-concealed glee that the number wasn't listed.

"Well, look here," I expect Dr Caetano said, "this is rather important. Between you and me there's this little coup going, overthrowing the President and that kind of thing . . . Well, it's sort of confidential and I'd be glad if you kept it to yourself but it is a teeny bit imperative that we get in touch with General Spinola."

"How many more times do I have to tell you", the operator no doubt replied triumphantly, "the number's not listed. Sorreee."

So much is speculation. But what we can be sure of is that some time later Dr Feytor Pinto was trudging round the streets of Lisbon asking passers-by if they could direct him to General Spinola's house and we all know what happens when you get involved with that sort of caper. The first person you approach inevitably says, "Sorry, old man, but I'm a stranger here myself. Perhaps *you* can help *me*. You don't know the way to Revolution Avenue, do you?"

"Revolution Avenue?" One can just see Dr Feytor Pinto wrack-

ing his brain. "I'm sure I passed it just now. I think it's back th . . . No, hang on, we'll ask this milkman."

The milkman removes his cap and mops his brow. "Isn't that daft? I know it like the back of my hand and yet it's gone right out of my head. You want Revolution Avenue, you say?"

"Yes," says Dr Feytor Pinto, "well, I don't – he does. Actually I want to find General Spinola."

"General Spinola?" says the milkman. "He doesn't live on Revolution Avenue."

"I never said he did," says the good Doctor. "I don't know where the hell he lives but if I don't find him soon he'll have my guts for garters."

"Hold on," says the milkman. "Come to think of it there is a Spinola on Revolution Avenue. Not a general though, is he? I always thought he was a piano tuner. Owes me two weeks' milk and half a dozen eggs . . ."

Incredibly, the General was actually found in time with what results we now know. But even so it's a pretty funny way to run a coup. And when you think of that and what happened in the White House, don't you find yourself wondering sometimes what on earth must be going on in Downing Street?

May 5, 1974

Wronger than Thou

I must confess to a certain ambiguity in my attitude towards all the apparent honesty and breast-beating that's going on in politics at present.

Margaret Thatcher began it, you remember, some weeks ago when she said the Tories had got it wrong last time they were in power. I can't remember exactly what it was she said they'd got wrong because, frankly, I didn't take much notice at the time. I thought it was simply old Maggie, notorious milk-snatcher, putting her foot in it again.

What will happen, I felt, is that Ted will have her, as it were, on the carpet and tomorrow she'll issue a statement saying everyone had got it wrong when they said she said the Tories had got it wrong. But no. I'd got it wrong. What happened, in fact, was that she received so much public praise for her candour that she set an astonishing trend. Suddenly there's a queue of politicians jostling for the privilege of telling the public what a monumental cock-up they made of it last time around.

Sir Keith Joseph, of course, got in first with his speech at Preston in which he challenged Tory economic policy as outlined by that dynamic duo, your friends and my friends, Mr Heath and Mr Carr. This was a subtle refinement on Maggie's prototype confession – Mark II as opposed to her Mark I.

He didn't say "I've got it wrong" or even "We've got it wrong" but "*They've* got it wrong", thus making it clear that when the Conservatives start thinking again about leadership it's no use looking towards Edward or Robert. On the other hand, and to show that he can be as fashionably fallible as anyone else, he added that unemployment was not half so bad as people believed, a statement so manifestly preposterous that any day now Sir Keith will be able to return to the television cameras and, scratching beneath his hair shirt with the other hand, announce triumphantly that he'd got it wrong.

The question that bothers me is: where will it end? And also: is it a good thing or a bad thing? Can an electoral stomach, sustained from infancy on whopping lies and insane promises, absorb and digest this terrifying new diet of frankness?

To put it another way: can we, before the election, look forward to a telly confrontation between our two sleek, plump, silver-haired leaders on these general lines . . .

Ted, sternly pebble-eyed: "I think I can say, and I'm sure the voters will agree, that in three and a half years of Tory misrule we plunged this country into such a parlous state as it had never known before."

Harold, puffing complacently on pipe: "Coom, coom, Ted, I can't let you get away with that. Even overlooking the utter chaos we created from 1965 onwards, I must point out that the present Labour Government has brought Britain closer to total bankruptcy than your lot ever did – and in months, not years, sithee."

Ted: "Nonsense! Who introduced the three-day week? Already you've forgotten the darkness, the misery, the cold and in some cases (dare I say it?) the near-starvation that I introduced, all by myself, in the early days of this year."

Harold, relighting pipe: "Old history, lad. Any road, who got the *Financial Times* index down below 200? Not your lot – took Labour to do that."

Ted, waving smoke way from face: "Ah, but who said he could control prices at a stroke and was proved wrong the very next day? Search your record as you may, you can't point to a mistake like that."

Harold, coughing: "Well, if you're talking about inflation, lad, we've got you beat hands down. Look at prices today, compared with prices only six months ago. Soared beyond recognition, they have. And what's more they're getting worse all the time – in minutes, not hours."

Ted: "Perhaps you've forgotten Tony Barber and the ludicrous budgets he introduced."

Harold: "Nay, good point, Ted. But remember Dennis Healey's doing a pretty lousy job there and we've still got him – you've lost Tony."

78

Ted: "What about Patrick Jenkins and shaving in the dark?"

Harold: "What about Wedgie Benn and almost anything he says?"

Ted: "Patrick Jenkin's dafter than Wedgie!"

Harold: "Rubbish! Nobody's dafter than Wedgie . . ."

With that sort of stuff coming out I can't really fancy the chances of Jeremy Thorpe and the Liberals. I mean, wrecking your own hovercraft on the beach is hardly in the same league, is it?

September 9, 1974

Rockies Horror Show

The American yeti expedition is gathering in Washington State again on the annual quest for Bigfoot, as he is known to his intimates. Over the years he's been frequently glimpsed in the Rockies and besides having enormous feet he resembles apparently a giant, hairy, primitive man.

Well, the expedition's looking in the wrong place, of course. They should come over here. They're bound to find him standing for Parliament somewhere, probably as a candidate for the National Front, although to be fair the National Front is the only party to have its priorities right.

The others simply fog the issue by chuntering on about the Common Market and the potential effect of distant relatives of Lord Emsworth deserting the Labour Party, while the passion has clearly gone from the inflation debate now Mr Healey's made it quite clear that everything's pegged at 8 per cent, no matter how indignantly Mr Carr might cry "Wubbish!" from the other side of Smith Square.

No, it was only the National Front that got down to essentials with this line in its manifesto: "We have enough that is rich in our own British heritage of song and dance not to require that imported Negro rhythms monopolise the mass media in the way that they very nearly do." There'll be none of that nigger music around when we of the National Front take power, I can tell you. There'll be no racially integrated *Black and White Minstrel Show* either.

For it's only when you think deeply of the debilitating effects of imported Negro rhythms on our British way of life that you realise the full implications of Mr Whitelaw's recent angry accusation that the Labour Party was going round the country "arrogantly stirring up complacency". It's not just the Labour Party, nor even the fact that here we are already facing the second "General Election of the Century", this year, that's whipping people up into a positive frenzy of complacency and driving them into the streets afire with blazing apathy. It's all those imported Negro rhythms blunting our senses and turning us into a race of pink-skinned Sambos.

If you look closely enough you'll find that imported Negro rhythms are responsible for the deterioration in the quality of our lives in almost any area you care to name. For instance, I read in a newspaper report only the other day that a lady in Shepherd's Bush had taken to offering her clients a line in "pseudo-masochism and bondage". Great Scott, I thought, what is the country coming to when a man in search of a little innocent masochism and bondage after a hard day's work can't even get the genuine stuff any more?

Still, you can see what must have happened. No doubt the lady was lolling about the house between appointments one morning, listening to imported Negro rhythms oozing out of her tranny and the insidious quality of this so-called music took its effect. "Ah, the heck with it," she said. "Masochism and bondage – who needs it?" And, swaying her hips and clicking her fingers in time to the imported Negro rhythms, she added the word "pseudo-" to her business cards, murmuring, "They'll never know the difference."

Oh, the signs of this baleful influence are everywhere. I mean, we of the National Front were appalled to learn last week that Harold Wilson had not, contrary to popular belief, been suffering from housemaid's knee but only from a wrench or strain.

We'd rather approved of Harold's having housemaid's knee because, naturally, we assumed he'd acquired it through clearing up after Lady Falkender when she put the cover on her typewriter at 5.30 sharp every evening. Beyond question she'd have left the floor littered with crumpled envelopes and the results of the false starts she'd made in typing Harold's acceptance of all those resignation letters from the House of Lords. And, obviously, she wouldn't have picked these things up herself because, as a member of a white-collar union, it wasn't her job. Therefore Harold would have had to get down on hands and knees and tidy up before she came in again next morning.

An honourable way, we thought, for an industrious prime minister to contract housemaid's knee. But a wrenched knee is another matter and it's our belief that he suffered that while jiving round the Cabinet Room with Lady Castle and Shirley Williams to the strains of imported Negro rhythms.

So there's only one answer to Britain's problems – vote National Front. You'll recognise the candidate at once. Big fellow, he is, sort of hairy, with large feet.

September 30, 1974

Happy Returns

If you asked me I'd say it was a *good* general election but not a *great* general election though my friend Bob wouldn't agree at all. Mind you, he's a bit partisan is Bob. His idea of a narrow Labour victory is an overall majority of not less than three hundred.

"Strewth!" he said, as the TV screen showed the early state of the parties: Con 2, Lab 0. "The game's hardly five minutes old and they're two up already. We've got to take Peterborough." He's been saying that since 1966. I don't know why. I think Peterborough's a kind of talisman for him. I think he feels, in some obscure way, that a world in which Labour can take Peterborough can't be all bad.

Anyway, we were having our usual election-night party, a fact of which my wife had reminded me that morning. "You will be back early, won't you?" she said. "Who are you lunching with?"

"Julian," I said.

"Oh, my God!" she said. He's a sort of guru of mine, this Julian: a splendid fellow and my wife is very fond of him but she regards him as a malignant influence on me, particularly on election days. She's never forgotten that in 1970, after a spot of premature celebrating with Julian and others, I fell asleep on the train and missed not only my own party but the entire general election.

So this time I phoned after lunch to tell her I was on my way. "Your voice is high," she said. (This is another gambit of hers; she keeps insisting that after the kind of occasion which leads me to fall asleep on trains I'm a dead ringer for a boy soprano.)

"Nonsense," I said gruffly.

"Don't fall asleep on the train," she said. I wish she wouldn't go on about that. You'd think I was always doing it, instead of . . . Well, there was one occasion, I must admit. Middle of the night, it was, and I woke up in some godforsaken spot miles away. She had to get dressed and come and fetch me and what made it worse was that when she caught up with me I was trudging along the road in the wrong direction, towards the Scottish border.

Still, my exploits on trains are nothing compared to her brother Roger's. Once he phoned from London to say he'd be arriving on the three-thirty. We went to the local station to meet him. He wasn't there. We went home again. The phone rang. "It's Roger here," he said. "I'm at Stevenage."

"What are you doing at Stevenage, Roger?" I said.

"Ah well, see, the train didn't stop at your station. There's one going back the other way in fifteen minutes . . ." We went to the station to meet him. He wasn't there. We went home again. The phone rang.

"It's Roger here," he said. "I'm at Welwyn Garden City."

"What are you doing at Welwyn Garden City, Roger?" I said.

"Ah well, see, this train didn't stop at your station either. There's one going back . . ." We went to the station to meet him. He wasn't there. We went home again. The phone rang.

"It's Roger here," he said. "I'm at Stevenage again."

"Don't tell me, Roger," I said. "See if I can guess. The train didn't stop at our station, right?"

"Yes, it did," he said, "only it was a very long train and you've got a very short platform and they wouldn't let me off . . ."

However, I didn't fall asleep on the train. I was still up and awake when Robin Day was having an early morning chat with Roy Jenkins and Robert Carr . . .

"'Morning, Woy."

"'Morning, Wobin."

"'Morning, Wobert."

"'Morning, Wobin."

"We've got to take Peterborough," said Bob and about then the Peterborough result came through, announced by the ubiquitous returning officer, Ivy Undersigned – and we all cheered. "We've got to take Sidcup," said Bob.

I finally got rid of him just after three. We hadn't taken Sidcup and Bob was about to throw my telly into the garden because they wouldn't show the figures at Welwyn and Hatfield. When he'd gone I went to bed and when I awoke the radio was on. ". . . and now over to Sidcup where we asked Mr Heath if the election result would affect his political future."

"Mr Heath, will the election result affect your political future?"

"Bluuuuurgh," said the radio. Or maybe it was Ted. I wasn't quite sure. Anyway, it seemed an appropriate comment. Yes, a good general election but not a great general election. I expect next February's will be better.

October 14, 1974

Viandes Roses

I think I'd better set the scene so you'll be able to appreciate the full horror of the moment. There I was, wandering about the Loire Valley . . . What? Well, no, not very nice actually. Rather cold, as a matter of fact and quite a lot of rain about. Sorry? Oh, the food. Well, now you're talking. One night I had this *truite aux amandes* that was absolutely out of this world – a delicate, tender fish obviously well brought up in a very good home and completely smothered in almonds. An excellent house wine with it, too: a crisp white Saumur, nicely chilled and . . .

Anyway, where was I? Oh yes, in the Loire Valley. Well, I'd been away a week, completely out of touch, hadn't seen a newspaper since I left England and as I passed this bookshop I looked round and there, on the rack, was an English Sunday paper and on the front page, glaring at me with his cold-eyed fanatical sincerity was Sir Keith Joseph and underneath the picture of Sir Keith was a story that made the croissant turn to ashes in my mouth.

How can I describe the impact of what I read? Well, I'll tell you: it was like walking into a darkened room, switching on the light and . . . "Oh, whoops, sorry Sir Keith. I didn't realise you were embracing Mrs Whitehouse." Dazed, I was. I believe – I can't swear to this because the shock has affected my memory – but I believe that opposite Sir Keith was a picture of Mrs Whitehouse smiling her cold-eyed, fanatical smile and I think he was quoted as calling her "an admirable woman", which is about as passionate as one remoraliser can be about another.

I wasn't surprised exactly. In its time the quest for remoralisation must have thrown together stranger bed-fellows than Sir Keith and Mrs Whitehouse. I was just sort of shattered because I'd had this wistful hope that they wouldn't actually find each other.

The events of the next few minutes are hazy in my mind. My appetite was gone, I know. I could no longer face the restaurant for which I was headed. I seem to recall walking, as one in a mist, to the fish market, mechanically buying myself a few oysters at 50p a dozen, a slice or two of *pâté de campagne*, a *baguette*, a bottle of wine and perhaps a morsel of cheese and sitting beside the Cher while I forced down this simple meal purely in the interests of keeping body and soul together.

It wasn't, you understand, that I objected to being remoralised. It was merely – so far gone was I in self-indulgence – that I didn't want to be remoralised by those two. Leaving aside his jokes about the birthrate and the light-hearted implication that the country will soon be overrun by plebs, shuffling creatures with low foreheads and apelike arms, swinging aimlessly from lamp-post to lamp-post while uttering low, gutteral cries, I couldn't honestly see that a programme of remoralisation headed by Sir Keith and Mrs Whitehouse would be a whole lot of fun.

Brooding thus over the stern Puritan atmosphere that surely awaited my return home quite spoilt my holiday. Oh, it's true that I continued to toy with a *coquille St Jacques au whisky* here, a *terrine de canard* there, the odd *escargot*, a steak *au poivre*, a plate of *moules farcies*, a dish of *tripes á la mode de Caen*, even some wild pig in Burgundy sauce with chestnut *purée* but my heart wasn't really in it.

To tell the truth, I was suffering from a sense of guilt. Sir Keith is quite right. This country has needed remoralising ever since the day, all those years ago, when the cynical Old Crofter told us we'd never had it so good. And what I feel is that if Sir Keith believes a policy of remoralisation can win him the leadership of the Tory party and possibly a future lease on 10 Downing Street then no doubt what is good for Sir Keith is good for the nation.

Already I'm setting my own modest example. I had a final light snack – some oysters and a bottle of Muscadet – before I left France and started remoralising as soon as I stepped aboard the British Rail ferry at Dieppe. I could have gorged myself on fried sausages, black as charcoal and afloat in fat, limp white chips, tinned peas and pre-sliced bread but firmly I denied myself these gluttonous pleasures. It may not be much but even in remoralising everyone's got to start somewhere.

November 4, 1974

Mother's Pride

> *Old Mother Hubbard went to the cupboard,*
> *To get her poor dog a bone.*

But when she got there the cupboard was sort of light on bones, being crammed with tins of salmon and tongue and corned beef and ham and mackerel and . . . Well, we knew all this stuff already. And if you happened to see the *Daily Mail* you'd know more about it than most because the *Daily Mail*'s always popping in and out of Old Mother Hubbard's kitchen, trying to borrow a cup of sugar, I daresay.

It was there the week before last, taking pictures of her washing up without even her pinny on. What I mean is that she was wearing a rather pretty dress unprotected by a pinny, which suggests that she's either not much accustomed to washing up or that she's a lot better at it than I am.

I always wear a pinny when I wash up because I believe in splashing about fairly vigorously, and if I haven't got a pinny on I get my jumper absolutely soaked. O.M.H., on the other hand, didn't seem to have a mark on her. She was holding up this spotless plate from which every vestige of the breakfast-time salmon mousse had been removed and saying, "I have been misunderstood, badly misunderstood", while no doubt the *Daily Mail* was clearing its throat diffidently and murmuring, "Well, it doesn't actually have to be a *whole* bag of sugar. I mean, whatever you can let us have would be much appreciated. Just until the supplies are back . . ."

Anyway, that was the week before last and several days went by before the *Mail* dropped in again, this time to photograph her in front of an open cupboard, frowning into the camera while pointing sternly at a jar of jam.

I don't know what the *Daily Mail* was after on this occasion but I don't imagine it can have been jam. Jam seems to be reasonably plentiful in the shops, so the situation probably was that the *Mail* was doing a bit of stocktaking and discovered it had run low on bread and somebody had said, "Look, why not drop in on Old Mother Hubbard? You know what she is – she's bound to have a spare loaf."

And, of course, this was perfectly right, because O.M.H. had stocked up with a full week's supply the previous Friday. So I

85

expect that while the photograph was being taken she was saying, "I'm not sure I can let you have any jam. As you'll see, I'm down to my last six jars", and the *Mail* was saying, "Well, ah, see we're okay for jam. We were wondering, you know, whether you'd got any bread. If you could just see your way clear to lending us a few slices of Mother's Pride . . ."

It must have been about then that O.M.H. delivered her good housekeeping tip: "If there are going to be days without bread the best thing to do is to buy unsliced loaves and store them in a cool place, then wrap them in a damp tea-towel or kitchen paper and pop them in the oven when ready for use." Well, I'll not argue with that, though it wasn't actually a whole lot of use last Thursday when most of us, less prudent than O.M.H., were jostling each other in the bread lines.

The interesting points that emerged, however, from the *Mail*'s neighbourly visits to the lady were these: first, as she pointed out, "My cupboard is not a hoard in any sense. It is a store cupboard." Note the subtle difference – not food speculation but food reclamation which, as even Harold would agree, is another matter entirely. And, second, her method: when she has used a tin or jar of some commodity she replaces it with two others.

Now clearly this must be recent policy and not, as most people have uncharitably assumed, the result of years of careful reclamation, since at present she has only six tins or jars of everything. On the other hand, if she carries on this way for another year or so she'll be better equipped than Sainsbury's while – according to current prognostications – the rest of us will be in the grip of an international food shortage such as we'd never envisaged.

That being so, we'll *all* be popping round to Old Mother Hubbard's in the hope of borrowing something and muttering, "Bless her thrifty heart." The queue, I can tell you now, will form on the right immediately behind the man from the *Daily Mail*.

December 9, 1974

Sink or Swim

If the bookies have got it right, the Tory Party can console itself with the thought that whether or not it ends up with a good leader it will at least have acquired an extraordinarily good wife.

You don't surely think it's coincidence, do you, that after all those cosy pictures of Willie washing up and Maggie sweeping the floor, the odds at the weekend were 5/4 on for him, roughly evens for her, and the rest nowhere?

They know a thing or two, those bookmakers, and what they're trying to tell us is that after ten abrasive years of manly bachelorhood from Atastroke, the Tories want a complete change. They don't want a stern disciplinarian who goes around kicking lame ducks; they want a comfortable, warm-hearted mother-figure with red, workworn hands, and baking powder on her nose who'll kiss the place and make it well.

Jim Prior has totally misread the situation. This is not a time for prancing about on the fringe of the battle like a catchweight Muhammed Ali, stinging like a butterfly and floating like a bee while shouting, "I am the greatest." In any event, there's too strong a sense of *déjà vu* about Muhammed Jimi: that silver hair, that plump frame, those rosy cheeks – don't they remind you of somebody? To see him enter the contest just as his former leader left it was like watching Atastroke walk out of the room only to discover he's still standing behind you.

Of course, Jim may well have argued that what the Tories were seeking was somebody who looked like Atastroke without actually being Atastroke, in which case he would certainly be their lad. But, as it transpires, he's ruined his chances by not putting in enough time in the kitchen.

Much the same might be said of Sir Geoffrey Howe and John Peyton, although the latter entered the lists for refreshingly individual reasons: "It's a crazy election system," he said, "but I'm getting on the bandwagon." Possibly he reasoned that if it was that crazy it might even be crazy enough to elect him although he didn't know his brass polish from his Omo.

No, only Willie and Maggie read the signs correctly, and now it just remains for the Tories to decide which of these two manifestly splendid wives would make the better wife.

Maggie has the edge in experience. We've seen more than enough pictures of her pointing proudly into a well-stocked larder, up to her elbows in the sink, slaving over a hot stove and, just the other day, down on her knees with dustpan and brush, very probably collecting the remains of the crockery she dropped while washing up.

Willie is a late contender in the housewifery stakes, and so far his repertoire seems to consist solely of washing saucepans with his shirt sleeves rolled down, and a bemused expression on his face. But, on the other hand, he's undoubtedly the more motherly figure of the two. Give him time and practice, and I imagine he'll be just as much an absolute darling about the house as Lady Elwyn Jones claims the Lord Chancellor to be. I have very little doubt that if he's elected he'll soon be able to take his rightful place in any gathering of international statesmen with detergent rash on his hands and his tie splashed with bacon fat, and swap recipes with the best of them.

The problem is, however, that when tomorrow – or maybe Thursday – the Tories choose one, and thereby reject the other of these two domestic paragons, they may cause a rift in the party. I think, though, that this can be avoided.

What I hope will happen is that if, say, Willie wins, he'll invite Maggie to his home and, greeting her at the kitchen door with a kindly and sympathetic smile, will thrust a tea-towel into her hands, saying simply "I'll wash, Maggie – you wipe."

"Willie," she'll say, "you don't mean . . .?"

"Yes, Maggie, I do. You're to be my deputy."

"Oh, Willie," she'll say, "with you washing and me wiping there's no limit to what the party can achieve."

Mind you, there's always a chance that Maggie will turn the whole election on its head by having herself photographed tomorrow morning lying under her car wearing crisp white overalls with a spanner in her hand and a becoming smear of grease on her forehead while she casually does a quick engine change, thus proving herself better man than any of the others. But I don't really think it'll happen. The slogan of this election campaign is: If you can't stand the heat, get out of the kitchen.

February 10, 1975

Lady Chataway

Great Scott, what's this? I mean, here on the front page of a daily paper: "Now I've nothing to lose by showing myself as I really am . . ." Mrs Thatcher talking.

I'm bound to say that I turned to the requisite inside page with much trepidation. True enough that a change in the supporting cast down at the Westminster Palace of Varieties had put new life into the longest-running show on earth – but there seemed a distinct indication in this titillating front page come-on that the entire production had been taken over by Paul Raymond.

Equally true enough, it had been made manifestly clear to us that Maggie was the Tories' Playmate of the Month, but what startling revelations awaited us on page thirteen? Full-frontal Thatcher baring all? Coyly abandoned poses in twinset and hotpants round the statue of Sir Winston Churchill? Off-the-shoulder Maggie, mean, moody and magnificent, draped all over Ted's old desk?

Well, in the event, it was just the usual stuff about "baby-blonde" hair, and blushes the colour of "light coral rose", and "You don't have to turn out like a sack to gain people's respect." Very disappointing really and no indication at all that she would listen sympathetically to an offer from Hugh Hefner.

But what with all this and similar revelations on the Jimmy Young Show: "I said, Reggie, would you like to join us again? And he said: 'I'd love to, my dear.'" And "My wardrobe is very small, one cupboard. I have to wear tailored things in fairly good plain colours", and "I haven't owned a twinset in years. I simply must

buy one." What with all this, I say, I'm beginning to wonder if somebody isn't missing the point.

Surely there must be more to the leadership of the Tory Party than this unbroken stream of light, feminine gossip. Look at it this way: assume the election had been on the other side of the House, and Harold had emerged as the new leader of the Labour Party. Would he then have approached Mr Callaghan, saying, "Wouldst tha like to join us again, Jimmy?" and would Mr Callaghan have replied "I'd love to, my dear", and would Harold have greeted this response with a blush the colour of light-coral rose, and dashed off to break the news to Jimmy Young?

Would he be caught patting his baby-soft silver hair and confiding to Jean Rook that it didn't matter whether he was a man or a woman, he wanted to be accepted for himself? Would the papers announce that he rose at six o'clock to cook Mary's breakfast before bustling away to break his own fast with Henry Kissinger, and would it be revealed that Mary stood at the door saying, "Will I ever see you again?" while Harold shouted back, "Happen not this week, sithee?"

Would Henry say, as they parted, "He's quite a boy", while photographers and gossip writers expressed disappointment that kisses had not been exchanged? Would Harold tell Jimmy Young that his wardrobe consisted of just a few tailored things in fairly good plain colours, bearing in mind that he had to consider what he would look like on a platform to those at the back of the hall, and also bearing in mind that he had to sit around and jump in and out of cars all day and still be dewy fresh at the end of it?

Well, I don't know. Till now I think that, had it been my place to do so, I should have strongly advised Harold against any of these activities. But at the moment I'm not so sure.

The latest opinion poll, taken while Maggie was in full spate of her girlish confessions, suggests that in a general election the Tories would have a 4 per cent lead over Labour, although all we've really learnt about the potential Conservative prime minister in the past couple of weeks is that she's a dab hand with dishcloth and dustpan, needs an hour off a week to get her baby-blonde hair tinted, had "a horrid day" sacking Shadow Cabinet ministers, and is privileged to call Jimmy Young by his first name.

And if that's enough to give her a 4 per cent lead, Harold's obviously on the wrong track. We don't want a prime minister who charges about playing the statesman and trying to negotiate £1,000 million deals with Russia. What we want is a prime minister who, if she plays her cards right, might one day end up in a public clinch with Henry Kissinger.

Kitchen Cabinet

Unfortunately I missed the television programme in which Mrs Wilson revealed that it was Harold who chose the menus for diplomatic dinners at No. 10 and I regret that because I like to seize every opportunity to learn about the personal foibles of the great men who lead us ever deeper into the mess of inflation.

However, I did study the reports of the interview and what Harold does apparently when he's drawing up a menu is to include everything that he likes and hope that everyone else likes it, too. If not, presumably, it's tough luck on them and lots of seconds for Harold.

But what Mary doesn't seem to have mentioned is exactly what it is that the Prime Minister prefers to eat. The only clue afforded was in a brief description of the culinary delight whipped up for Mr Shastri when he was Premier of India: a hard-boiled egg, a lettuce leaf and a glass of water.

Now come, come, Mary, I said to myself on reading this. Nothing will convince me that what Harold likes best for his dinner is a hard-boiled egg and a lettuce leaf. You don't get to be Harold's shape on a diet of hard-boiled eggs and lettuce leaves. But, of course, the explanation came in the next line. A hard-boiled egg and a lettuce leaf wasn't what Harold ate; it was what Mr Shastri ate. Harold had something far more succulent and drank wine with it, too.

Well this struck me as odd because, in my experience, when one is invited out to dinner one is not usually obliged to pick at a weight-watcher's snack while one's host fills his boots. But what happened, I expect, was that Harold came home from the office that day, slapped Mary on the rump and said, "Ayoop, lass, into t'kitchen. Old Shastri's coming to dinner."

"Mr Shastri? Isn't he the Indian gentleman?"

"Aye, Mary, so I'm reliably informed."

"But, Harold, what on earth am I to give him to eat? I'm hopeless on curries."

"Curry? Who said owt about curry? You know I don't like curry. Any road, you can't give curry to a starving Indian. Rip his guts up, that would."

"Starving? Are you sure Mr Shastri's starving, dear?"

"Bound to be, lass. They all are out there. Jim Callaghan told me so."

"Well, I'm sure I don't know how Jim would know that. He's never been to India, has he?"

"I don't know where he's been, sithee. He's not a man to boast about his travels. But he does know about India. He gets it all from an Indian conductor he met on the No. 11 bus."

"That's all very well, Harold, but it doesn't solve the problem of what we're going to eat tonight."

"Don't fuss thissen, lass. Leave it to me, like always. What I suggest is a good dish of Lancashire hotpot and jam butties for afters. Right, well that's me settled. Now, what about old Shastri?"

Some hours later Harold, Mary and Mr Shastri are seated at the festive board and Harold is helping himself copiously to the hotpot.

"My goodness gracious me," says Mr Shastri, licking his lips, "it is many, many years since I am eating the Lancashire hotpot."

"Happen it is," says Harold, chewing sympathetically. "Too rich for the old tum now though, eh? Never mind, Shastri lad, we've got summat special for thee . . . Where's that daft butler gone? Wedgie! Bring in Mr Shastri's dinner at once."

Enter Wedgie, the butler, to place before Mr Shastri a hard-boiled egg and a lettuce leaf. "There!" says Harold. "My idea, that were. Eat hearty, lad. I bet that's the first square meal you've seen in months. A good English hard-boiled egg that is . . . well, Polish actually. They're cheaper this time o' year . . . and if you fancy another lettuce leaf, just sing out. Rabbits will have to go short for once. Wedgie! Bring in the Japanese burgundy and pour Mr Shastri another glass o' water."

Later still Harold kicks off shoes, sinks into armchair with a sigh and undoes top trouser button. "By gum, that were a good nosh, lass. I think old Shastri enjoyed it, too. Did you notice? There were tears in his eyes when Wedgie put that hard-boiled egg in front of him. Poor starving devil."

"Yes. Funny that he didn't stay very long, though, wasn't it, dear?"

"Wanted to get home to watch *Kojak* I expect, same as us. Any road, happen that third lettuce leaf did for him. Mistake to stuff thissen when you're not used to it. Switch on t'telly, lass . . ."

April 7, 1975

3

This Sporting Life

Britain's Putty Medals

The Olympic Games had barely begun before that familiar sporting phenomenon, the Plucky British Loser, has made his mark; not too firmly, because in the Winter Olympics we lose in such an utterly total and British way that, plucky though we are, few of us take part. Nevertheless, we were there at Sapporo, plucky, British, and defeated, our attitude epitomised by Squadron Leader Mike Freeman, bobsleigher and flag-bearer: "We may not be the greatest at winning Olympic medals but at least we can carry our bloody flag properly."

Indeed how true. But while we prance about showing the world how flags should be carried, sneaky non-British competitors beat us out of sight in the events. Not that we care; we admire our losers. "A fine performance by this British girl", says the TV commentator, shrill with excitement, as the triumphant British girl finishes forty-ninth or thereabouts in the downhill races.

Furthermore, the Olympic P.B.L. has hardly got into his stride yet. He will not be at his most glorious until Munich when, game to the last, he struggles home in twelfth place, a lap and a half behind the unfancied Wog, Wop, Frog, Hun or Gyppo who has actually won the gold medal. "Fantastic!" everyone will cry. "What courage, what pluck . . ."

It is the same in all sports, of course, we never loved our footballers more than when, in their plucky British way, they achieved the almost impossible feat of losing to West Germany in the World Cup after being two goals ahead. No doubt this is all very commendable. It is not the winning but the taking part and all that stuff; and certainly the British example of how to lose gracefully is a byword, largely because, having had more practice at it than anybody else, we have developed it to an art form. Even so we have surely produced more than our share of decent, smiling, modest losers. How nice if, just once and just for a change, we could unearth some scowling, arrogant, sullen, morose, evil-tempered, self-opinionated and gloriously un-British winner.

Guardian *Leader Column*
January 8, 1972

Dream Culture

I can understand that Sotheby's must have been slightly cross with the eccentric gentleman who bid £255,600 for nine Old Masters and then, when they had been safely knocked down to him, confessed – cheerfully, I hope – that he had no money at all and couldn't even begin to pay for them.

The fact that, on being re-offered, the same paintings fetched £104,000 less may well have caused Mr Peter Wilson, the chairman of Sotheby's, to rush off home and kick the cat.

Nevertheless, my sympathies lie with the penniless bidder. How splendid for him to know that, if only for a few moments, he had outbid all the dealers, collectors, investors and general fat-wallets and owned nine (count them, nine) Old Masters.

I was not present, unfortunately, to witness the event but I can imagine it . . . Mr Wilson up there on the rostrum with his busy little hammer – "Do I hear 50,000?" Yes, he heard 50,000 all right. "60,000?" Yeah, what the hell, 60,000, why not? A stir in the crowded, stuffy room, all eyes on the mystery connoisseur at the back, fanning himself gently with his catalogue and wondering why so much fuss was made about auction sales when all you had to do to collect Brueghels and Canalettos was nod occasionally at that nice Mr Wilson.

It was a question, I like to think, of a man having the sheer nerve to make a wild dream come true. In America, Mr Ron Galella had a dream, too.

He wished to take a photograph of Mrs Jacqueline Onassis wearing hotpants and the fact that Mrs Onassis never wore hotpants did not deter him from this simple aim.

Of course, Mr Galella's motive was rather sordid and commercial. He wanted to sell the picture for a vast sum of money. But even so you have to give him grudging credit for persistence. When Mrs Onassis unreasonably refused to don hotpants for him, or even to let him photograph her at all, he tried to sue her for $1.3 millions, alleging that she was ruining his livelihood.

It's arguable, I suppose. If you insist that your profession is "Jacqueline Onassis photographer" and Jacqueline Onassis won't play ball, it could be quite a long time between meals.

But the point about both these men – and the essential difference between them and the rest of us – is that they were courageous, or thick-skinned or just plain daft enough to try to give substance to their dreams. Not, alas, I.

About this time of year I like to turn up at Trent Bridge or some such ground and win the Ashes. It makes no difference what kind of player England needs, I am the man for the occasion. An unplayable slow bowler? I flex my spinning fingers and dismiss Jim Laker from his place in the record books. A batsman capable of scoring 200 before lunch? Look no further, Illy, I am here.

But unlike Mr Galella, I don't actually sue the England selectors for not picking me, nor – in the manner of the man at Sotheby's – do I simply arrive in the dressing-room with my gear and tell the likes of Boycott they won't be needed.

This is partly, I admit, because I'm a bit ashamed of my gear. Apart from an elderly bat that has been oiled to the texture of balsa

wood, it consists of a pale-blue baseball cap, a pair of Indian batting gloves, a jockstrap with no elastic and the only piece of equipment that I regard as totally indispensable, namely a box.

Powerful though my daydreams are, I have enough grasp of reality to know that, thus attired, I should have some difficulty in getting out of the pavilion, let alone on to the pitch.

In the long run, no doubt, one's chance of seeing those innermost yearnings take tangible shape depends very largely on who one is. The most notable Walter Mitty of recent times was that bloke in the yachting cap who conned the L.S.O. into letting him conduct them, merely because he purported to be running the country, a preposterous claim that, incredibly, went unchallenged.

The orchestra was very nice to him but if he had been anyone else it could, at worst, have kicked him out or, at best, have actually followed the movements of his baton with God knows what result.

Life is real and life is earnest and the world can be very hard on dreamers – unless you've got a bit of pull, that is.

July 17, 1972

Games People Slay

Well, actually, I'm glad those Africans have gone. I mean, I ask you – fancy pulling out of the Olympic Games on account of their principles, as if principles had anything to do with the Olympic Games.

Besides, it's damned embarrassing. If anyone withdrew because of the Rhodesian contingent it should have been us. We're the ones with a grudge against Rhodesians, after all, and if we're prepared to let them take part with mock-British passports you'd think those uncouth Africans would shut up, wouldn't you?

It was left to dear old Avery Brundage to put them in their place. "We don't want politics in sport," he said, sitting on the beach like King Canute with the water lapping his chin. You can't help liking him – one of the few genuine innocents left in the entire world.

There he goes now – see him? A trusty old bloodhound, nose twitching, hot on the trail of some despicable shamateur with a running-shoe manufacturer's contract in his pocket. That's it, Avery – sic 'im, boy!

We, in Great Britain, are on his side, happily. Didn't we, at a stroke, clear all the alleged pot smokers out of our team, even going so far in our zeal to keep the Olympic flame of purity burning brightly as to expel one wretched lad who was prepared to swear on the Bible, his bended knees and, if necessary, his mother's life, that he wouldn't know a stick of grass from an ear of corn?

Avery will certainly approve of that, as will the athletes from other nations as they gather in their respective parts of the Olympic village and pass a joint around among themselves to soothe their nerves.

Nobody, however, will approve more than the wrestlers, weight-lifters and shot, hammer and discus throwers gulping down their ration of steroids and lurching about, gargantuan and creaking with muscle, like a chorus of chief eunuchs in a musical remake of *The Thief of Bagdad*.

Anyway, now the Africans have dropped out it gives us a better chance – our lot, British and plucky, that pale, fragile-looking, white-clad bunch over there, an object of curiosity to all the other competitors because, by and large, they really are amateurs, either by choice or because our running-shoe manufacturers are a good deal meaner than other running-shoe manufacturers.

Without a horde of fanatically fleet-footed spades to contend with, you never know, we could do much better in the heats and even in the finals. We could finish seventh out of seven instead of eighth out of eight.

And that sort of success might take some of the pressure off poor David Bedford, who will be treated as though he had committed an act of treason if he doesn't win the 5,000 metres or the 10,000 metres, or both, despite the fact that though he may be a brilliant runner against the clock he is not necessarily a brilliant runner against other brilliant runners.

But, of course, what the African absence really means is that the U.S. and the U.S.S.R. (with attendant satellites) will be able to compete against each other for the important medals without tribes of impudent emergent black people getting in the way.

The Americans, as usual, will be represented by career college boys, many of whom after no more than a decade at university have the dazzling ability to read simple words without moving their lips and jot down their names in joined-up writing with hardly a spelling mistake.

Against these intellectual giants will be ranged the proud sol-diery of Russia (and Poland and East Germany and the like), skilled and dedicated fighting men, among whose number are those who could, if called upon to do so and given a few clues, identify a tank at five paces, and others who know that to order arms you don't necessarily have to present a requisition slip to the armourer.

All these, naturally, are genuine amateurs and therefore making a far better living than genuine professionals– as witness the case of Tommy Smith who won a gold medal and gave the Black Power salute at the last Olympics and, being understandably ostracised, has lately been reduced to training no-hopers in the north of England for his bread.

We don't want people like him or other committed wogs in the Olympic Games, thank you very much. We want genuine Simon

Pures who wouldn't dream of making political capital out of the fact that America won more gold medals than Russia, or vice versa. They're only games, you know. They're not World War Three. Well, not yet.

April 21, 1972

Stung to Action

It was, of course, absolutely typical that the only competitor in the entire Olympic Games, so far as I know, to have been stung on the bum by a bee was British.

Mind you, I suppose it was predictable. Had you been told, prior to the event, that any moment now a neatly jodhpured bottom would descend on a slumbering bee which, understandably indignant at such a liberty, would strike back in the only way it knew how, and had you been asked to guess the nationality of that bottom you would have said, would you not, without a moment's hesitation, "Oh, British, naturally."

After several days of largely unscheduled disasters – British canoeists capsizing as if that were the object of the exercise and swimmers vanishing without trace into the deep end – to be attacked by bees was about all our team needed.

Admittedly, if you must look on the bright side, it could be argued that only a British competitor, afflicted thus with such a bizarre wound, would still have had the fortitude to get up on her horse and finish seventh. Even so, it had to be one of our lot, didn't it? It couldn't possibly have happened to anyone else.

You don't hear of Mark Spitz getting stung on the bum by a bee. Nor Shane Gould. Nor, come to that, the precocious Russian gymnast, Olga Korbut, who was so enchanting and sweet and graceful and lovable and adored by the crowd that by the end of the week I felt like giving her a damn good kick.

It's so unfair, not to say depressing. As the Games enter their last week I can't help wondering, with much trepidation, what other indignities fate holds in store for us, the best of British luck being what it is.

Actually, I think I know what will happen. As our runners round the final bend in the 5,000 metres, side by side and half a lap ahead of the field, they will all disappear down a manhole, never to be seen again.

In the matter of these Olympics I've now worked out where my sympathies lie. Oh, with Britain, of course. I'm as good a jingoist as the next man – but Britons apart I don't care where the competitors come from, what colour they are or whether they've given up beating their wives.

All I want to know is: how old are they? Once that's established I know which has my support – that one there, the one the commentator just called a veteran.

It took me a couple of days but I finally reached this conclusion when the boxing commentator mentioned a "veteran" Russian, a veritable Methuselah of a pugilist, apparently, a man so old he could actually remember the Mexico Olympics.

"I dunno," the commentator said, doubtfully, "perhaps his age is just too much for him to carry." Well, for God's sake, how old could he be? I put on my reading glasses and knelt before the telly, trying to work it out. He didn't look that old to me but then neither do policemen these days.

Finally, the extraordinary news was broken to us. This poor, decrepit hulk carrying his nation's colours in the boxing ring was every bit of thirty.

Thirty! Can you imagine? What are the Russians doing, sending out these old chaps to do battle?

All right, yes, sport is a young person's thing. But Youth's getting a little short these days if one girl arouses awe by winning a medal at twenty-one and another is "almost a veteran" gymnast at twenty-five and a European champion is a grand old man at thirty.

September 4, 1972

Join the Club

Golf, as every right-thinking person will agree, is a thoroughly boring game except possibly when played by Laura Baugh. Rain having washed out play at Lord's, the TV cameras switched to the Ladies' European Open at Sunningdale and I tuned in just as Miss Baugh was trying to hit her way out of a bunker with a wood.

What a glorious shot! Did you see it? – the tossing blonde hair, the graceful sweep of the arms, the pulsating sweater, the glimpse of softly rounded midriff, the plump tightness of jeans over swinging hips. Beat that, Nicklaus, I cried, overcome with admiration for this ancient game.

The fact that the ball hit the lip of the bunker and rolled back to Miss Baugh's feet is neither here nor there. This girl doesn't need a ball to make golf the most exciting spectator sport in the world. All she needs to do is stand in a bunker and swing.

I was so carried away by the sheer eroticism of it that, until wiser counsels prevailed, I was very nearly tempted to take up the game again myself. I haven't played for years, of course, but there was a time . . .

Well, I was initiated in it by my friend Neil, a beginner himself though you'd never have known it. The way he threw his number-nine iron at a tree after missing a chip shot, well, you'd think he'd been playing all his life.

I was a quick learner though. And an innovator. It was me who introduced jumping up and down on the golf bag *and* throwing your putter into the water hazard. Pretty soon I knew nearly as many wrinkles as Neil.

I even took golf lessons. "Swing," said the pro. "It's no good saying 'Here's me head, me arse is coming.' Swing!" Anyway, I caught on fast and the day when, aided by a natural slice and a following wind, Neil hit four consecutive balls into the A1, I matched him shot for shot. That would have been a pretty tight game if we'd ever finished it but all of a sudden we heard these motorists climbing up the bank from the road, shouting things, and Neil said he didn't care to continue the round if they were going to let that sort of rowdy element on to the course.

There was, however, one shot of his that I was never able to equal and that was when he was driving off through a gap between some trees. Encouraged by his slice the ball hit the trees on the right, ricocheted off into the trees on the left, back to the trees on the right and . . . "Look out!" said Neil and threw himself to the ground. That was the only time in my experience when a man's tee shot actually ended up behind him.

It took me ages to find Neil's clubs after that. I had to climb a tree to get one of them and Neil was no help because he was kicking his ball all the way back to the clubhouse.

Pretty soon afterwards the weather got cold and I gave up golf. But the next spring a friend asked if I'd give his fourteen-year-old son his first lesson. "Watch me carefully, lad," I said and hit a rather good drive about seventy-five yards and only just into the rough.

"Like this?" said the kid and POW! his tee shot went a clear 220 yards down the middle of the fairway.

"You're getting the hang of it," I said, the smile never touching my eyes, and went to find my ball.

I was a bit inspired that day. It only took me three more shots to catch up with him and in fact I believe I created a personal record by breaking a hundred for the first nine holes but somehow my heart wasn't really in it.

"I can't see what you're doing wrong," said this ratty kid, as I came as near as dammit to sinking a ten-inch putt on the twelfth. He marked his own par four and moved off. I don't know how he completed the round because it was hard to see the fairway from the long grass and his father had taken him home by the time I'd four-putted the eighteenth.

I've never played golf since. Never wanted to either. A kid's game, I thought it was – until Laura Baugh brought this whole new set of dimensions to it and revived my interest. I wonder if she and I could get together and swap tips on things to do in bunkers.

August 12, 1974

Waiting for a Pay-off at Bert's Palace

Selhurst Park
Crystal Palace: 0   Norwich City: 2

If Bert Head were playing Monopoly, someone remarked with more wit than charity, he'd buy the Old Kent Road instead of Mayfair. Not true at all. He started the week by trying to buy Mayfair (assuming Ted MacDougall at £220,000 can be so described), but Frank O'Farrell landed there first.

Mr Head may have finished up with a package-deal of three lesser properties at £280,000 the lot, but it would still be unkind to liken them to the Old Kent Road, begging Millwall's pardon, of course.

As it happened, only one of the new Palace acquisitions, Iain Phillip (£110,000 from Dundee) was on display, since Paddy Mulligan (£75,000 from Chelsea) was poorly with a sore throat and Charlie Cooke (£85,000 from Chelsea) was ineligible. Thus Mr Head was in the frustrating position of a gambler limited to putting only a third of his stake on the table. "Don't equate today's result with the £280,000," he said afterwards. "It's not fair."

Palace had been played on to the pitch with much canned music – though not, oddly enough "Hey, Big Spender" – and the record of having failed to score in their last six matches.

This distinguished run they stretched to seven without any trouble at all. A flick over the bar early on by Craven, an optimistic thump by Hughes, an even more optimistic scissors kick by Craven again and two or three uninhibited long-range drives by Hinshelwood were about the best they could muster.

Yes, said Mr Head later, you could say Palace were still in the market for another player. A striker? "Call him what you like," said Mr Head. "Some bugger who puts the goals in anyway."

Norwich, actually, were quite well equipped with buggers like that. Bone scored the first after twelve minutes, a corner and a scene of total chaos in the Palace penalty area. Fifteen minutes later Paddon got the second, amid similar panic, with a header.

Meanwhile, Phillip – neat but not gaudy – was dividing his attentions between Bone and Cross and doing quite well. His colleagues treated him with polite reserve, as though they hadn't been formally introduced yet, and rarely gave him the ball. He shouldn't feel too slighted by that, however, since they rarely gave it to one another either. "Phillip?" said Mr Head. "He'll be all right once he's settled down and sharpened up. The lads were a bit disjointed today. They'd lost confidence, don't believe in themselves any more."

On the whole, though, he was encouraged by the thought of the players he'd signed. "Not a bad week's work," he said. "Of course, I'm still a bit sore about MacDougall, but he's gone so there's no point in talking about him, is there?"

True, but it was a lot of money he'd spent nevertheless. Didn't it worry him, gambling all that on three players? "It's the way prices go, isn't it?" he said. "Of course they're ridiculous – a £100,000 transfer is nothing these days. It's like bananas – they used to be two-a-penny, but they're not any more. No, I'm not worried, though. You back your fancy, that's all. It's the occupational hazard of being a manager. The day I lose any sleep through worry is the day I pack it in."

On the field Norwich had skated the first half and eased up a little in the second when, to do them credit, Palace did look somewhat more businesslike. Even so, just before the end the slow handclapping started, somebody waved a banner saying "Head Must Go" and Bone came off, being, in the elegant phrase of his manager, "knackered".

So once again Palace are in their familiar position near the bottom of the league. "Well," said Mr Head, "we're in the process of building traditions here. I didn't buy these players on a short-term basis, just to get us out of trouble. If you're spending that much money you have to think long-term. You have to think of getting into Europe, otherwise it takes years to get the money back."

In any case, he said, though he's invested £750,000 in players in the last four years he has got most of it back by selling others. "Anyway, look at it this way: if I spend half a million pounds this season, which I might, it'll seem an awful lot. But I may not spend any more for another five years. You have to judge it, not week by week, but over a length of time."

Palace, I said, haven't done all that well in the First Division. Wasn't he, perhaps, a little disappointed? "I'm not disappointed to be here," he said, "if that's what you mean. No, you make your own problems just by getting into the First Division. Managing any club is hard – it's a lot harder in this league. Besides, we've got four players to graft into the team – Cooke and Mulligan, and Mel Blyth and Tony Taylor, who were injured today."

Cooke, clearly, should make a difference, since what Palace lack, apart from the ability to score goals, is someone with flair who can hold the ball and use it intelligently. Mulligan, too, should tighten the defence, which yesterday at least was involved in one unscheduled disaster after another in its own penalty area.

Mr Head is naturally aware of this. "I'd settled with Cooke and Mulligan before I even went after MacDougall," he said. "So I certainly didn't get them in place of him. What we need now is a goal-scorer. Once we get one and get over this bad patch, I think we'll be terrific."

He was not, then, feeling in any way desperate?

"We're never desperate here, mate," he said. "We're never desperate here."

Crystal Palace: Jackson; Payne, Roffey, Kellard, Phillip, McCormick, Pinkney, Craven, Jenkins, Hinshelwood, Hughes.
Norwich: Keelan; Payne, Butler, Govier, Forbes, Briggs, Livermore, Bone, Cross, Paddon, Anderson.

Observer
October 1, 1972

A Dash of Humour, a Touch of Pride and a Love of Cricket

The ball from David Brown, of Warwickshire, that brought a temporary halt to Geoffrey Boycott's run of mammoth scores inflicted a double indignity upon that great man, for, on its way to damaging his eighth rib, it flicked his glove and then, rebounding lustily from his heart, was caught. Mr Boycott takes up the tale himself . . .

"When I got back to the dressing-room one of the Yorkshire lads said, "Did that 'urt thee captain?"

I said, "Aye, it did. But Ah wish it 'ad 'it me straight on t'bloody 'ead or in t'teeth instead."

He said, "Tha' wouldn't ha' looked so good wi'out teeth, captain."

I said, "'Appen not, but Ah wouldn't ha' been bloody out, though, would Ah? Ah could ha' got up and got me bloody 'undred."

This story, recounted in the deliberately exaggerated Yorkshire dialect so brilliantly captured above, tells us two things about Geoffrey Boycott, the first of which we knew already – namely, that he doesn't like getting out.

("Listen," I said, "here's the situation: you're batting on a terrible wicket against an extremely fast bowler. Now be honest, aren't you ever frightened of being hurt?" He looked at me in deep wonderment, as though doubting whether I could be serious.

"The only thing I'm bloody frightened of," he said, "is getting out. I don't like getting out. I bloody don't. I like getting hundreds.")

The second, and less familiar aspect of Boycott's character revealed by that anecdote is that he is a dryly amusing man with a pleasing sense of humour. This comes as a shock to the interviewer meeting him for the first time, because Geoffrey Boycott isn't supposed to have a sense of humour. He's supposed to be a remote, withdrawn man, icy and taciturn, interested exclusively in his own achievements and glory.

It is, I think, because of this widely accepted, though erroneous, image that he often gets considerably more stick and correspondingly less praise than he deserves.

He wasn't the only England player to turn down the tour of India, but he was the one who attracted the adverse publicity. He's the one who gets the blame for the fact that Yorkshire win very few batting points, although, as someone pointed out, "Just look at the scores – there's Boycott with 150 and the rest 70 between 'em."

Last summer he was much criticised when he declined to play in the last Test against Australia and people implied that he was scared of Lillee. "Well, all right," he said, "I admit it– I was bloody scared, but not just of Lillee. I was scared of anyone above medium pace right then.

"I'd been out for six weeks wi' t'top o' me bloody finger 'anging off" (his Yorkshire accent becomes very strong in moments of passion) "but nobody mentioned that, did they?"

"They didn't mention that I wasn't scared of Lillee when I hooked him twice on that rotten pitch at Manchester and hooked him again off his full run in the One-day Test."

He believes himself to be misunderstood by the media and therefore misunderstood by the public at large, and it makes him unhappy. He is not, he insists, the remorselessly dedicated monster he is made out to be. He loves cricket, that's all; that's why he tries so hard.

Nor is he the crazy egomaniac of popular myth and legend. True, he can give you the exact details of every innings he has ever played, but he doesn't hurl the statistics about in a boastful way. He uses them rather, as a defence against those who seek to belittle him.

He's a proud man: proud that he captains Yorkshire ("the leading cricket club in the world") and proud that he plays for his country. He will never tell you that he's a great player, but he knows it all the same – and why not? Only a fool or a churl would deny the fact.

But he feels that the British are ungenerous to their great players. "None of 'em's appreciated till he's retired or dead," he said. Nevertheless, he's not paranoic, doesn't feel himself persecuted and can well understand how his fortunate image came to exist.

"When I started in this game", he said, "I must have been a godsend to writers looking for copy. I was a very rare bird in cricket in those days – a young man who didn't smoke and didn't drink, who was shy and introverted and found it difficult to talk to people, who was mad keen on physical fitness and who liked batting so much that he'd go to the nets even when he didn't have to.

"Oh, aye, I must have seemed a right crank. And on top of it all, I wore those rimless glasses that made me look like that bloody fellow Himmler."

Still, he says, that was a long time ago and he's changed a bit since. "Okay, I've got a lot of confidence in myself– sometimes. Not always. I need support and encouragement and warmth. I'm a very emotional guy. I'm supposed to be cold and calculating – sphinxlike, they call me, but I'm not like that at all.

"I don't show emotion much, but inside, if the crowd is with me, I'm on fire. I play emotionally. In Yorkshire the crowds are fantastic; they really appreciate me, and when I'm batting up there it's tremendous. I want to get runs not just for Yorkshire, not for myself – but for all those people who are willing me on to score more and more.

"It isn't just a cricket pitch any more . . . it's like an arena, it's my stage and I'm like an actor and the people have come to see *me* give a performance, I wouldn't swap it for anything."

Indeed he *is* an emotional man and a friendly one; over-sensitive, perhaps, and easily hurt, but also engagingly honest and open. He talks with almost boyish fervour of the big moments of his life, like the frightful day when, at seventeen, he learnt he had to wear glasses and thought his chances of a sporting career were over.

In despair he wrote to M. J. K. Smith, that bespectacled rugby and cricket international ("and a marvellous bloke") for reassurance – and got it.

Just to round the story off, when G. Boycott went on his first tour of England, his captain was that same M. J. K. Smith and, just to round the story off even further, M. J. K. Smith couldn't remember the correspondence.

Boycott also talks of the time he was picked, to his own total astonishment ("I'd never thought I'd be good enough for England") for his first Test – against Australia in 1964.

"I remember nothing of that match," he said. "It was like a dream, wonderland. It was only days later that I suddenly woke up to the fact that I'd played for Yorkshire *and* England. Me! I'd played for my country. It were fantastic."

Actually he does remember one thing, very clearly, about that Test, and he tells it with much relish and amusement.

"As I went out to bat in the first innings, Bobby Simpson, the Australian captain, threw the ball to the fast bowler Graham McKenzie and said in a loud voice, 'Hey, Garth, look at this four-eyed cuffer! He can't cuffing bat. Knock those cuffing glasses off him right away.' And I said to myself, ''Ello, Ah thought we'd coom out 'ere for a nice game o' cricket. Ah didn't know it were a bloody war.'"

Good bloke, Geoff Boycott. When Illingworth gives up, he should be England's captain. I don't suppose he will be though – too much the pro, too much the "bloody Yorkshireman" and not enough the gentle amateur that the selectors seem to be seeking as Illy's replacement.

But if Boycott doesn't get the job, I suspect it will be much more England's loss than his.

Observer
May 13, 1973

Fair Kop

Chief Superintendent Harry Shelley, who is responsible for policing Derby County soccer ground, said last week that footballers who played dirty should be booked by the police and risk the possibility of prosecution in the courts.

Right – over now to Jimmy Hill and *Match of the Day* . . .

"Good Evening. With me tonight is Tom McBrawn, one of Britain's greatest and most respected football managers. Tom, I thought the lads did well today, considering you finished the match with three men on bail, three at the nick and one in protective custody."

"Aye, Jum, there's real team spirit buildin' up at the club the noo, although there are still some who are no' pullin' their weight. It's a sad reflection on the game that four o' my players can come through ninety minutes o' hard fitba' wi'out gettin' theirsel's booked by the referee, let alone cautioned by the police."

"Well, you're a perfectionist, Tom. But what I'd like you to do now is talk us through the game. Excitement started when the whistle blew even before the kick-off and if we look at the slow-motion replay we can see who blew that whistle. Yes, there he is – that uniformed policeman at the Kop end. You remember the incident?"

"Och, aye, Jummy. That was when our skipper got arrested for assault wi' a deadly weapon, to wit, a fitba' boot. But, ye ken, he didnae try tae kick the referee at all. He was just tryin' tae maim Kevin Keegan but the ref got in the way. And, incidentally, Ah was very disappointed at the ref taeday – always interferin' wi' the play, never lettin' a real pattern emerge. Look at the time our winger went in wi' a cripplin' tackle on Steve Heighway an' the bloody ref got in the way.

"It ruins the game as a spectacle when the play's constantly interrupted because the trainer's tryin' tae revive the ref. And Ah must add that if the ref hadnae been on the blind side o' the police that tackle on Heighway would hae been worth a month in Pentonville for our lad."

"Ha, ha, marvellous the way you stick up for your boys, Tom. The tackle wasn't really worth much more than a heavy fine and a suspended sentence. Still, how about your skipper – only just back to football after a week in Wormwood Scrubs for common assault on Norman Hunter. Aren't you afraid of losing him again?"

"Och, no, Jummy. Ah dinnae think the referee will be able tae give evidence. He's still in a coma after getting' in the way again when our striker tried tae butt Phil Boersma. So, wi' any luck, the lad could get awa' wi' probation."

"Well, Tom, we don't have time to consider all your seven heroes individually so let's just take your centre-half. What a blinder he played, right up to the moment he was frog-marched off the pitch by the riot squad. He's coming up for G.B.H. on Ray Clemence, I believe."

"Aye, Jum. What happened was that he was testin' out his theory that Clemence has a weakness against crosses."

"Crosses from the wing, you mean?"

"Nay, Jum – crosses to the jaw. When he jumps tae catch a ball he leaves his chin unprotected – a bad fault in a goalkeeper. Sae, when we got that corner, my lad was in wi' a right tae the jaw an' a followin' left under the heart. Beautiful tae watch, it was. He'll get a month at least."

"Finally, Tom, your own goalkeeper's in protective custody tonight?"

"Ae, Jum. He did a silly thing – tried tae frame Alec Lindsay but he's too inexperienced tae do it properly. Fancy expectin' the fuzz tae believe it was Lindsay who kicked Emlyn Hughes in the jock-strap – his ain team-mate! Tempers got a wee bit strained on the field sae Ah asked the police tae take the lad into protective custody."

"In case the Liverpool players came after him mob-handed?"

"Och, it was nae but a precaution, Jum. The Liverpool players are too soft – the season's two months old already and there's no' one of 'em's seen the inside o' a cell yet. Ye cannae hope tae win the fust division wi' form like that."

"Well, Tom, I shan't keep you any longer because I know you have an important appointment."

"Aye, Ah have, Jum. Ah'm off to meet oor centre-forward. He's just been released frae Dartmoor after servin' time for the attempted murder of Martin Peters at White Hart Lane."

October 7, 1974

Grandmother Clock

Let me put it this way: I don't know whether Granny Dakin of Worcestershire was, or was not, guilty of the "ungentlemanly conduct" that got her banned from the Stourbridge football ground. She says she wasn't and I'm certainly not here to dispute the word of a granny and a gentleman.

Nevertheless, something obviously occurred at the Stour-bridge-Weymouth match: fingers were raised in V-signs, heated words were exchanged, a rattle was brandished and some-body (not Mrs Dakin, apparently, but her daughter – a potential granny worth keeping an eye on) threw a punch at a former Welsh international fullback and when the dust had cleared sixty-year-old Mrs Dakin was banned from attending future home matches.

I don't know how you react to all that but I feel curiously cheered by it. It seems to me that simply by being involved, whether she participated or not, Mrs Dakin has done wonders for the virile image of grannies everywhere. Can there indeed be a granny in the land who didn't feel the blood coursing more freely through her varicosed veins when she read of the exploits of Granny Dakin?

For too long now grannies have been undervalued members of society – frequently living alone, neglected by their own kith and kin and existing on pitifully inadequate pensions. Governments ignore them because they have no power to withdraw their labour, the very word "granny" is often used as a pejorative and literature hardly makes mention of them.

In Australian slang, according to the invaluable Eric Partridge, "granny" is even a synonym for "nonsense". Of course, one could expect no better of an uncouth tribe that recaptures the Ashes by the despicable expedient of having a first maniac bowling very fast at our gentle batsmen from one end while a second maniac effs and blinds at them from the other. But even in the Bible the most notable reference to grannies is the warning in the Table of Kindred that a man must not marry his grandmother.

Apart from anything else, that superfluous piece of advice always reminds me of my favourite line in my favourite bad movie, *Zarak* – the bit when Victor Mature is standing as close to his stepmother, Anita Ekberg, as her magnificent boobs will allow and whispering – or from that distance, I suppose, bellowing – "It is written that a man must not marry his father's wife."

Besides, you'll notice that in the Table of Kindred the granny inevitably cops the passive role. Why not write it the other way around – "a woman must not marry her grandson" – thus acknowledging that even a granny can experience the odd pang of illicit lust?

No, it was time the granny image was refurbished and by the publicity she has attracted Granny Dakin has certainly done her bit. I'm not, you understand, advocating that grannies should turn their hands to violence – bad enough when the sub-human yobboes (prototypes of Orwell's proles) who support Manchester United and Chelsea create terror on the terraces and set fire to railway carriages.

We certainly don't want rampaging hordes of soccer-mad grannies descending mob-handed on our football grounds, all-black bombazine, iron-grey hair and nutcracker jaws, laying about them with their brollies and putting the elastic-sided boot in on lone, inoffensive grannies who happen to be waving their rattles on behalf of the opposing team.

But at least we have now been reminded that grannies, too, can have fire in their bellies, that they're not lightly to be shoved around and that when the battle is at its fiercest there's a pretty good chance that a granny will be somewhere around in the middle of it.

With this knowledge still fresh in the public mind the time has come, surely, for grannies to organise, to show the full extent of Granny Power, to demand an International Grannies' Year. Instead of wasting our time extolling the dubious virtues of dough-faced blondes in non-events like the Miss World contest, we ought to have a Granny of the Year competition.

Furthermore, I don't wish to see it won by some freak granny who achieved the noble status at the age of 33 merely because she and her daughter both managed to conceive at the earliest age compatible with the law. I'd like the title to go to some real tough, knock-'em-down, drag-'em-out, spit-in-your-eye granny. I repeat: it's not clear on existing evidence whether Granny Dakin falls into that category, but she'll do for me. I nominate Granny Dakin.

January 20, 1975

Test Case

The House of Commons voted last week to appoint a Select Committee to investigate the curious behaviour of a group of Englishmen who disappeared from these shores several months ago, and mysteriously turned up some time later in Australia, purporting to be Test-match cricketers.

Urging these men to return home and help the Committee in its findings, Mr Edward Heath said, "This House understands full well the weaknesses and frailties of our fellow human beings. And the House is widely known to be compassionate and understanding in very difficult personal matters of this kind. I believe they would have no justifiable fears about receiving fair play and justice."

In Australia, however, it is believed that it is the very fear of receiving fair play (and particularly justice) that is making the alleged cricketers extremely reluctant ever to return home at all.

And indeed, even in the House of Commons, Mr Heath's view – though fully acknowledged as revealing the generosity of spirit, not to mention compassion and understanding which he traditionally brings to bear in his relations with everyone save coal miners and Mrs Thatcher – is regarded as excessively charitable.

General opinion is about equally divided between, on the one hand, destroying the runaway Englishmen's birth certificates, cancelling their passports, tearing down their houses, burning them in effigy, deporting their families, and declaring them and all their friends prohibited immigrants, and, on the other, bringing them back forthwith to face not so much justice as retribution.

Already the Director of Public Prosecutions has drawn up warrants for the immediate arrest of every member of the party, each of whom is alleged to have committed offences under the Trades Description Act, and some of whom will face the far greater charge of unlawfully impersonating an England batsman.

The evidence of their culpability is believed to be contained in a thick dossier of newspaper reports from various Australian cricket grounds, each of them headed: "Day of Shame for England". For the moment, though, Mr Edward Short's contention that a squad of armed policemen with orders to shoot on sight should be sent to Australia to bring the men back dead or alive, is felt to be a little extreme.

In any event, experts who have been following the bizarre exploits of the Englishmen on television have advanced the theory that they are not so much criminals as men in urgent need of psychiatric help.

The opinion of these experts is that the party has suffered a collective mental breakdown, the most characteristic symptom of which is a pronounced nervous tic which causes them all to flail wildly at any ball passing harmlessly outside their off-stump. This view is also shared by a Mr Ian Chappell, who is among those who have followed the group's eccentric progress around Australia with ever increasing bewilderment.

"Anyone could see at the first glance", said Mr Chappell in an exclusive interview with our Adelaide correspondent, "that not one of the flamin' no-hopers had the faintest idea how to play cricket. But it wasn't until the first Test when they all started looking for sanctuary behind the square-leg umpire that I realised the poor flamin' Poms were in a state of total nervous collapse."

Curiously enough, during their first weeks in Australia the Englishmen nearly succeeded in their daring – though as we can now see ludicrous, to say nothing of pathetic – masquerade. But they were eventually exposed by an undercover fast bowler named Lillee who lulled them into a false sense of security by leading them to believe that, owing to a back injury, he could toil not neither could he spin. Mr Lillee was greatly assisted by his friend, Mr Thomson.

Last night as the Select Committee continued its investigation there were strong indications from Australia that some members of the group, who have already smuggled their wives and children out there, were about to seek political asylum and apply for jobs as postmen. On hearing of this, Mr John Stonehouse said, "If that lot stays here I'm swimming back to Miami."

STOP PRESS: It has been reported in some quarters that the man in charge of the English party is a Mr Alec Bedser. Solicitors for Mr Bedser have, however, issued the following statement: "Our client is a highly respected and bona fide retired Test cricketer. As such he wishes it to be known that far from being responsible for the group of imposters at present touring Australia, he has been deceived as much as anyone by their delusions of grandeur. Anybody suggesting otherwise will be sued for everything he's got."

February 3, 1975

4

Scenes from Domestic Life

Spare Room in the Big House

As the attractive blonde girl said, it gets quite lonely at home sometimes: "All those big rooms . . ." Lonely, perhaps, but not terribly quiet. "My young brother plays football in the corridor." How different, you might think, how very different from the home life of our own dear Queen. Well, yes, but wait a moment. As a matter of fact, this *is* the home life of our own dear Queen.

The blonde girl in question is Princess Anne, who was twenty-one yesterday and the above remarks are from a short film, *Princess Anne and her Children*, which is now touring village halls and libraries on behalf of the Save the Children Fund, of which she is president. What she says in it conjures up some odd fantasies about the domestic style of the folks in the big house at the end of the Mall.

For a start, presumably, there is the Princess herself wandering lonely, and even lost, from one huge, deserted room to another. "Mum? Dad? Charles? Oh, where the heck is everybody?" In another part of the Palace, Prince Andrew and Prince Edward are playing football.

"Okay, Ted. You're Georgie Best and I'm Chopper Harris."

"I'm always Georgie Best, just because I'm the smallest. Why can't I be Chopper Harris and thump you for a change?"

Above their heads there is a constant rumbling sound but they take no notice. It's only their father exercising his polo ponies in the corridor upstairs. "Right, dear. That coat and your handbag are the goal posts. It's the last chukka, ten seconds to go and the score's 2–2. Now here I come to get the winning goal." Canter, canter; gallop, gallop. Thud! "Ooh, sorry luv – look out!"

In the excitement nobody hears the cry of "Geronimo!" outside the window as the Prince of Wales, practising parachute jumps, hurls himself off the roof into the goldfish pond. And meanwhile, back on the ground floor, Princess Anne ("Mum! Dad! Chaar-lee!") has just walked into yet another vast and empty room. On the whole it sounds like fun. Well, quite fun. More fun than you could have in a semi, anyway.

Guardian *Leader Column*
August 16, 1971

As Safe as Spouses

The Institute of Life Insurance in New York has announced that married men are healthier, longer-lived and more contented than single men – an outrageous statement that must be treated with the deepest scepticism.

Quite clearly the whole thing is blatant propaganda dreamt up by the wife of some insurance chief after her husband's unmarried friend had come to dinner in a Lamborghini, with a showgirl on each arm.

"Gee," the insurance chief doubtless muttered, wistfully, as the guests departed in search of wicked and delicious pleasures, "old Hank sure has a great time." Whereupon his wife handed him the wiping-up cloth, saying firmly, "Homer, Hank has no idea how discontented he really is."

The next day the entire Institute of Life Insurance was driven into action, drawing up a report designed to prove to Hank (and most of all to Homer) that married men have got it made and they'd better believe it.

Hence, of course, the statistics. Statistics are endlessly impressive and very hard to challenge. Nevertheless, I suggest we look closely at those provided by the Institute of Life Insurance. What they claim (and I think I've got this right) is that married men are five times more contented than single ones. Aha, you ask, how can anyone measure contentment?

Well, I'll tell you: an investigator from the Institute of Life Insurance inveigles himself into the home of a married man and, after tossing down a few lobs to find his length, delivers himself of a vicious top-spinner. "Would you, sir," he asks, "say you were less contented, as contented or more contented than a single man?"

Naturally, the unhappy victim attempts to play this one off his pads, knowing that the implacable, blue-rinsed fielder crouching there at forward short-leg will snatch up anything that comes off the edge of his bat.

"Ah, yes," he says, "well . . . Hrrrmph. Er . . . I would say I was quite as contented as a single man. Aren't I, my dear?"

The fielder shuffles in closer. "More contented, my love," she says. Of course, he sees the danger and jabs his bat down defensively. "Oh, yes, quite, to be sure. That's what I meant – more contented. Isn't that right, my precious?"

"*Much* more contented, my sweet."

"Yes, yes, certainly. *Much* more contented, much, much, much more. Wouldn't you say so, my darling?"

"I'd say, my dearest, that you were at least five times more contented than any single man."

"Right, right! Of course. That's precisely what I was trying to say. Put me down, will you, as being five times more contented than any single man?"

Commenting on this report, an insurance spokesman in London, an obvious married man who, on his wife's instructions had gullibly swallowed the entire findings, said that married men enjoyed these benefits because "they're cared for in their homes".

Oh, really? By whom? A married man who lives not a million miles from where I sit was phoned at nine-thirty the other morning by a bachelor friend who apoligised gravely for disturbing him so early in the day.

"That's all right," said the married one, "I've been up since seven."

"Seven!" said the bachelor. "Whatever for?"

"Well, it was half-past six, actually. I got the tea, you know. For my wife and daughters. And fed the dog and cats. Then I went back to bed and had a lie-in till seven."

"Good grief," said the bachelor, remorsefully, "I must be interrupting your breakfast."

"No, no," said his friend. "I got the breakfast ages ago, I'm just washing up now."

"Look here," said the bachelor, "assuming your incredible story to be true, the rest of the day is surely your own?"

"Oh, yes," said the married man. "Until I get home from work, of course. Then I have to get the meal. For myself, you know, my wife, my mother-in-law . . . Anyone who's about, really."

You find this hard to believe? It's true. Furthermore, the wife of this married man has just informed him that his experience confirms the discoveries of the Institute of Life Insurance.

Being up betimes, she says, keeps him healthy and long-lived and being so incredibly busy that his feet hardly touch the ground leaves him no time for such luxuries as discontentment and wondering what he's missing.

Incidentally, the Institute's report also says that married women are healthier, longer-lived and more contented than single ones. Very probably. But how much healthier, longer-lived and contented are they than married men? Has any institute the courage to tell us that.

March 26, 1973

Vat Now?

My wife has just gone out to buy an electric food mixer, an enormous machine for which we shall have to take out a second mortgage and the necessity for which was, apparently, become a matter of extreme urgency.

I found this hard to grasp at first, since she has existed all her life without a food mixer of any kind save a cheap Continental one which isn't earthed and which she regards with such deep suspicion that she won't use it except when wearing rubber gloves and Wellington boots.

"I'm going to use the food mixer now," she announces, gravely, every few months, dressed as if about to go to sea on a trawler and showing the solemn calm of one who knows that, should the worst happen, her affairs are in order. "Keep out of the kitchen."

Actually, this is sound advice although not quite for the reason she puts forward. I always avoid the kitchen when the mixer is in action because the bowl is too shallow and bits of partly mixed food tend to fly around like flak.

She, on the other hand, seals the room because she suspects the unearthed machine of constantly spitting out lethal, though invisible, doses of naked electricity.

However, it looks as if the incumbent mixer is to be declared redundant and the reason, of course, is V.A.T. My wife recently discovered that this new model, the one she suddenly covets, carried no tax, being classified as an industrial machine.

It will, therefore, unlike other mixers, be more expensive from now on. "Think", she said, setting off to get it, "of the money we're going to save."

"On the other hand," I said, viewing the problem from the obverse side, "think of the money we're going to spend."

Spending money to save money, she believes, is to make money work for you. Nor is she alone in this. As the building societies reported last week, people everywhere have been drawing their cash and going on a spending spree.

I, alas, am in no position from which to contest her theory, since my one attempt at V.A.T.-beating has been a dreary failure. Several weeks ago I summoned a man bearing samples and ordered from him new carpets for about half the house.

Unfortunately, I'd not taken into account the fact that British carpet manufacturers, like British manufacturers of almost anything else, are always deeply astounded when somebody actually orders any of their goods and invariably shake their heads and suck their teeth and point out that as they're providing a commodity for which there's virtually no demand there'll be a delivery hold-up of several months, if not years. So I'll have to pay the rotten tax anyway.

My wife's argument, carried to its logical conclusion, would be that, had we been sensible, we should over the past few weeks have bought everything readily available that was likely to go up in price after V.A.T.

The house would then be full of caravans, three-piece suites, saucepans, buckets, pianos, electric organs, night storage heaters, power drills, sanitary towels and toilet paper and we should have saved hundreds of pounds.

My argument would be that, true, we should have acquired these things and saved all that money but we should also be bankrupt. This reflects, I suppose, the essential difference between the optimist and the pessimist.

Mind you, I could have suggested that if she waited until V.A.T. was imposed she could buy an ordinary domestic food mixer and still save. I didn't bother because I knew what her answer would be: domestic mixers are cheaper than the other kind and so, by not saving so much, we should effectively be losing money.

"Well, but look here," I said, just before she left, "why do you need a heavy-duty, industrial food mixer?"

"Oh, lots of reasons," she said. "For one thing it'll be marvellous for making cakes."

This, to be sure, was not at all a bad answer except that nobody in our house eats cakes, as a concession to my weight problems, I being the original comparatively thin man within whom there is a fat man constantly trying to get out.

The last time my wife made a cake was several Christmases ago and it was a very nice cake indeed. The only minor flaw was that she ran out of space while decorating the top, so that the slogan it bore read: "A Merry Xma".

When I suggested she mix up a bit more icing sugar to write: "And a Happy Impetigo" around the side she ordered me from the kitchen with a marked coolness and abandoned cake-making from then on. Still, I can see that with this new machine "Let them eat cake" will be the slogan of the house and the fat man within me will come leaping out, drooling with greed. V.A.T. is going to have a great deal to answer for.

April 2, 1973

Winter Whine

Yes, I did have a nice Christmas, thank you very much. I gave this party on Boxing Day. Well, I give one every year. I get a lot of plonk and boil it and throw in all kinds of mixed spices and stuff and people come from miles around to drink it up.

They tell me it's a very nice party, although I wouldn't know about that because I hardly see any of it. I'm stuck in the kitchen in my pinny and a cloud of steam like Macbeth's three witches rolled into one, muttering incantations over a bubbling cauldron.

Every now and then I venture forth with a jug in each hand to refuel the thirsty, weaving my way between people standing back to back, and shoulder to shoulder as they murmur seasonal greetings at each other in a confidential bellow.

No, I don't know how many people turn up but it is a great many more than even a slum landlord would bear to pack into a single house. This year I found one chap crushed into a corner against a bookcase apparently performing an act of levitation. He'd been there for an hour, he complained weakly, as with trembling hand, he proffered his empty glass above the heads of the crowd around him, and his feet hadn't been able to touch the ground yet. Could I possibly do anything to help him? No. I couldn't, I said, I had all these other glasses to fill, you see. I don't wish to give the impression that, except by those in dire need, I am ignored at my own party. My friends are extremely kind to me. "For heaven's sake stop and talk" they shout as I stagger by. But I don't have time. There are all these strangers who need replenishing. At my party there are always strangers, house guests of friends, people I've never seen before and will never see again.

They nod to me courteously as I top them up and then turn their backs. After all, they haven't come to a party in order to talk to a serving man in a pinny, have they? "I wonder where the host is?" they inquire of each other. "Well, as a matter of fact . . ." I begin and they look politely in my direction.

"What?" they say. And then noticing the jugs in my hand, they lift their brimming glasses saying, "Oh, no, thanks very much. I've got plenty for the moment."

This year as I emerged from the kitchen on yet another errand of mercy I overheard one such lady departing early, thanking my dentist for having permitted her to come to such a lovely party. He was remarkably gracious about it; said it was nothing at all really and if she'd enjoyed herself that was sufficient reward for him, and she must be sure to come again next year if she happened to be in the neighbourhood.

Of course, you may wonder why even I, saintly though I am, should be nice to quite so many people every Boxing Day and the truth is that I never intended to be.

My original plan, formed years ago, was to have a mere handful of friends in for a drink. But unhappily my wife is afflicted with a chronic disease which impels her, whenever we have a party of any kind, to invite everyone she can think of. Those of us who know her well are aware of this and do our best to restrain her.

For instance, just before we got married, she had the 'flu and, being delirious, insisted that she could see little people. "Oh my God," said her mother, "don't invite them to the wedding."

On that occasion she must have taken the advice because I don't remember them turning up. On the other hand, I think she got her own back by inviting them to our Boxing Day shindig. There's no other way I can account for the crowd. And the ironic thing is that, even if I wanted to, there is nothing I can do about it now. Our Boxing Day party, I am repeatedly assured, is part of Christmas tradition. It's a terrible responsibility, you know, being part of someone else's Christmas tradition.

December 31, 1973

Shot in the Dark

My wife is rather enjoying the present crisis but then she was better

124

prepared for it than most; certainly better prepared for it than I was.

Well, you know how it is. I wander around in this happy daze, reckoning that if I've got enough work to keep me off the streets and enough money to keep me off the dole life can't be all that bad.

As a matter of fact, being the kind of sybarite who has no objection at all to being warm and well fed, I quite liked the age of affluence and materialism which we abandoned for ever last Thursday afternoon when the Mighty Atastroke waxed wrathful with his people and, performing one of his economic miracles, plunged the whole country on to the breadline. It came as a shock to me, I can tell you. I mean, a three-day working week *and* my tell programme off the air. It's a bit thick.

My wife, however, took it all very calmly. There's an unfortunate puritan streak in her that has long ago made her suspicious of all this wealth and good living. "Mark my words, we'll pay for it," she used to say, spreading gloom like some soothsayer saying a fearful sooth. "Life shouldn't be this easy."

Anyway, as I said, she'd seen the crisis coming ages ago. To show you just how percipient a woman she is, she saw it coming way back in the good old days when there were trains. She had this table, you see, that she wanted to send to her brother on the south coast and she asked the railways if they'd carry it for her. Well, naturally, they wouldn't. What did she think they were – some kind of transport business? But they did suggest, if only to get her off the line, that their road-services department might oblige.

She got on to a very nice man in the road-services department and he said, "Certainly we'll take your table, madam, but I warn you – it'll get damaged."

Well, she didn't mind that – the odd scratch or two; after all it was a second-hand table. "No, madam," he said, "you don't quite understand. When I say it'll get damaged, I mean it'll get smashed."

"Nonsense," she said. "Smashed? Why should it get smashed?"

"Because, madam," he said, patiently, "things always get smashed. Everything like that gets smashed. If I were you, I'd try Pickfords."

"You know," said my wife, thoughtfully, "there's something wrong with this country." A shrewd assessment fully borne out only a week or so later when the entire nation found itself up to its eyes in the raw material for methane gas because a comparative handful of men refused to work overtime.

Soon after that, of course, there came the spectre of Atastroke laying his curse on his people and the following morning I found my wife making out her shopping list. "One shotgun," she muttered. "Double locks for doors and windows. Baked beans. Disinfectant."

"Hold on," I said. "What's the shotgun for?"

"It's for you," she said. "So you can go shooting."

"Oh, yes?" I said. "And what am I going to shoot – gangs of marauders trying to get at our baked beans?"

"Exactly," she said.

"Well, when do you expect them then?"

"You never know," she said, darkly.

"I see," I said. "And the disinfectant – I suppose that's in case of plague?"

"Right," she said.

"Do me a favour," I said. "When this house is besieged by marauders carrying plague and trying to steal our baked beans, hand me the shotgun and I'll shoot myself."

And yet, on second thoughts, I think she has a point. With Atastroke and the unions locked in a battle to the death and the Dreaded Barber stropping his razor ready to do a bit of bloodletting this afternoon, I have this vision of Christmas, 1974, when the countryside is littered with rusting trains and motorcars, I.C.I. has filed a petition in bankruptcy, people all over the land are crawling out of their homes in abandoned coalmines and power stations in order to dig up the motorways and find some earth in which to plant 'taters and in the crumbling remains of what used to be 10 Downing Street an emaciated Atastroke is croaking proudly, "We never gave in to the bastards, did we?" We'll be all right, though, my wife and I, with out baked beans and our shotgun.

December 17, 1973

All for Lawn

This is the time of year when I blossom forth as a keen non-gardener. I have a friend who is just the same and we meet occasionally over a glass of sherry to compare notes on all the gardening we have not done.

"Mowed your grass yet?" I say and he shakes his head slowly.

"Not yet," he says weighing his words carefully the way we countrymen do. "Bit damp for that, lot of heavy dew about you know."

We carry our glasses to the window and admire the rich, luxuriant pasture beyond which the top of his garden fence is dimly visible. Somewhere out there his lawn mower lurks, poised for action just as it has been since it ran out of fuel last October.

Other times we meet at my house and wander up and down the path prodding things with sticks. "Nettles coming on well," he says.

"Ah," I say, falling easily into the countryman's vernacular, "finest crop of nettles in Hertfordshire."

"Same as every year," he says. "Don't know how you do it. Thinking of making nettle wine again?"

"Ah," I say. I've been thinking of making nettle wine every year for at least a decade but it's not something you can rush into; you've got to wait till the nettles are ready for it.

Suddenly he points with his stick. "Good Lord, what's that?" he says. And we stumble through the grass to where a single crocus has burst through, a lone lawn crittur that has struggled bravely for life only to find that everything has gone contrary with it.

"You've been planting things," says my friend, accusingly.

"No, no," I say. "One of the kids must have done it." Decently he accepts this apology and we drink our sherry with the contented glow of non-gardeners whose work is still undone.

We've always been ahead of our time as non-gardeners, my friend and I. Once, under combined uxorial attack because the grass was obliterating the view from the window we put forward the idea of plastic lawns which would need no attention save an occasional hosing down. It was greeted with little enthusiasm but a year or so later plastic grass was on the market. If only we'd gone ahead with our scheme we'd have been rich men by now.

On the other hand, the true non-gardener never goes ahead with schemes. He dreams occasionally, of how nice the garden would look if only someone would cut the grass and plant the odd bulb but finally he waits for somebody else to do it and oddly enough somebody else usually does.

For instance, my friend phoned one day to ask, embarrassedly, whether he could borrow our lawn mower. His wife had put him up to it, of course. She'd gone down to the end of the garden and, having forgotten to blaze a trail, had taken hours to find her way back to the house. By now his lawn mower had vanished completely, hence his request to borrow ours.

"Take the mower round to John will you?" I said to my wife. So she did. And naturally he couldn't start it, so naturally she showed him how and, naturally, he kept stalling the thing so naturally she mowed his grass. The sight of her shoving the machine through the wilderness was too much for him and he had to go indoors and lie down.

Oh, yes, I think a lot about not gardening at this time of year. It was, in fact, about this time of year when I was a teenager, that I first discovered I was a born non-gardener. My parents were going away for a couple of weeks and my mother said, "See that bare patch in the lawn? Put some grass seed down, will you. There's a bag of it in the garage."

So, like a dutiful son, I hauled the bag out of the garage, prepared the ground according to instructions, sprinkled stuff liberally here and there, and retired. When my parents returned the rest of the grass was knee-high but the bare spot was still there, like a patch of alopecia on an unkempt head. "You didn't plant the seed," said my mother.

"Yes, I did," I said. She swept out of the house, returning a moment later with a bag in her hand.

"See?" she said. "Here's the grass seed – still unopened."

"Ah," I said, "what was in that other bag?"

"Earth," she said.

"Then that's what I planted," I said.

April 15, 1974

Ale and Farewell

"Shall we", I asked my wife the other day, "have an election-night party? Ask a few friends round, get a few bottles in and watch the match on telly?"

She delivered herself of one of those snorts that wives are so good at – a rude but not inelegant sound that suggests horror, disdain, repugnance and an amused contempt for the entire male sex. I think their mothers teach them how to do it.

"An election-night party?" she said. "After the last time? You must be joking."

"Oh, well," I said, "the last time, I mean, goodness, that could have happened to anyone, the last time could."

"Tell you what," she said, relenting a little, "we could have an election-night party if you promised faithfully not to turn up at all."

Actually, I'd forgotten the last time – 1970, do you remember, when there was still food in the shops and the average working man hadn't even begun to dream of a four-day weekend and Atastroke was going to stop the rise in prices and be such a Firm and Fair prime minister that the nation would be rendered utterly ungovernable in less than four years?

Well, anyway, we gave an election-night party that time – not too large because this was a period when the Socialists in our village could hold mass meetings in the telephone box at the crossroads.

It was a gesture of defiance, really. The result was obvious and we wanted to crow over the Tory across the road who had outwitted us in the matter of election-poster display because he was a long, thin fellow who could climb higher up the telephone pole than I could.

However, as it happened there was another party that polling day. A secretary at the office was leaving to get married and we could hardly allow her to embark upon this dubious venture without benefit of alcohol.

Well, you know how it is at a leaving party. You can't go until you've bought a round and if you buy your round early you still can't go because everyone else says, "You can't go – I haven't bought a round yet."

So one round followed another and then I said, "I'd better buy a round" and they said, "No, you bought the first one" and I said, "Well, I'll just buy another before I go" and someone else said, "If we're going round again it must be my shout next" and some time later I found myself sitting in a train feeling inexplicably overtired. According to mythology, newts, I believe, sometimes get as over-tired as I was.

The only cure for this distressing ailment, as I'd discovered in the past, is to close your eyes and meditate upon the state of the world. Now when I meditate in those circumstances the trance into which I enter is almost indistinguishable from sleep and I might easily have meditated all the way to Scotland had not the lady beside me somehow insinuated her shoulder under my head and kept jerking it up and down.

I got out of the train in unfamiliar surroundings and found a phone box.

"Where the hell are you?" said my wife.

"Hang on," I said, "I'll ask someone."

"Oh, God," she said, when I told her. "Well, I'm bloody well not coming to fetch you."

"It's all right," I said. "There's a train going back the other way in half an hour."

Some time later I arrived to find lights blazing in the Tory stronghold opposite (in those unenlightened days before Firm and Fair government we didn't have to Switch Off Something – Now) and a strange despondency among the few people still left at my party. Furthermore, on the telly there was a sort of puppet with vast teeth and eyes like stones.

"Switch over," I said. "I want to see the election result."

"This is the election result," they said. "That's the new prime minister."

"Nonsense," I said. "Does Harold know about this?" But they had folded their tents and stolen away, and the urge to meditate had come strongly upon me again.

The next day my wife was in a bleak, unresponsive mood that matched my own unaccountable malaise. I attributed her condition and mine to the election result and sought comfort at Lord's where Gary Sobers scored 183 for the Rest of the World against England. Even the thought that good old Enoch would have him expatriated before he could do it again afforded me curiously small consolation. It just wasn't my election somehow.

February 25, 1974

True Story

The Wilkins family of Reading, Berks., are to star in a twelve-week documentary series about themselves on BBC television and I only hope they know what they're doing. A few years ago the Loud family in America underwent a similar ordeal and when the dust had cleared the parents were divorced and their son had gone to New York to pursue his lifelong ambition to be a homosexual.

Of course, it's possible that the Loud marriage was already headed for the rocks and the son was at least an apprentice homosexual before the TV unit moved in. Besides, in this free and easy age you may say that divorce happens in the closest of families and Gay Lib will certainly demand to know what's wrong with being a homosexual anyway, to which I, being a liberal, hastily reply, "Nothing at all, though it's not necessarily what every mother wants for her son."

However, I dare say the Wilkins family, having been carefully chosen from fifty applicants, are made of sterner stuff and better able to cope with the business of being filmed night and day and with the nationwide celebrity that is bound to follow.

Even so, and without knowing a thing about the Wilkins lifestyle, I view the approaching series with some unease. A series that sets out to portray the "difficulties, hopes and disappointments, pleasures and opinions of an average family" must, if it is to carry out its brief, show everything or it might as well show nothing.

So I have this vision of episode one opening on a darkened bedroom, the camera slowly zooming in on two heaving mounds beneath the blankets, the microphone picking up their whispered conversation . . .

"Oh, go on. Please! Just this once."

"No, I don't want to. I don't feel like it."

"Oh, you never feel like it, do you, in the mornings?"

"No, I don't. Evenings, now, that's different . . ." The whispering grows softer but more urgent. Suddenly there's a muffled expletive and . . .

"Oh, all *right*! Anything to stop your nagging. *I'll* make the bloody tea."

From the bed emerges a disgruntled, bleary-eyed, puffy-faced, yawning man in unmatched pyjamas, scratching his belly. "Blimey," he says, "I've got a mouth like a navvy's armpit."

"Serves you right," says the mound under the bed-covers. "I'm not surprised, state you were in last night. Drunken pig. Hurry up with that tea."

The point is, you see, that family life is at best an undignified business. Family life is getting into a bath and having your wife and daughters hammering on the door insisting that it's absolutely imperative that they all clean their teeth now, this very second, and for goodness' sake hurry up and let them in.

Family life is getting out of the bath and discovering that the only towel in sight is dripping wet. Family life is being handed the hair lacquer instead of the anti-perspirant and crackling every time you raise your arms.

Family life is finding nothing in your drawer but seventeen odd socks and hysterically accusing your wife of harbouring a one-legged lover. Family life is realising, at the worst possible moment, that where the toilet roll should be there is only a tube of cardboard and stamping on the floor and shouting "Will somebody bring up the loo paper?" and, when the problem has been resolved, emerging to find eight of your wife's best friends drinking coffee and regarding you strangely.

Family life is your two-year-old daughter standing at the garden gate with your jockstrap round her neck and your cricket box on her head engaging the vicar in polite conversation.

You disagree? You don't believe me? "How different," you say, "how very different, from the home life of our own dear Queen – or, indeed, our own dear Wilkins family"? Well, possibly, but I wouldn't bet on it.

The details may change from one household to another but basically family life is merely a series of minor embarrassments – minor, that is, until you invite the TV cameras in to record them all for posterity and the edification of the nation at large. Bad enough, surely, to go to work knowing that you have a hole in your under-pants but how much worse to go to work knowing that all your mates know that you know that you have a hole in your underpants. It behoves us all, I think, to commend the Wilkins family for their courage and wish them the best of British luck.

March 18, 1974

Crumpet Voluntary

The most poignant phrase of the week was surely inspired by the plight of the *Q.E.2* which, poor old dear, was "drifting slowly and unable to make water" – a painful malady, God knows, whose diagnosis must have evoked a twinge of sympathy in the bladder of many a noted personage.

President Nixon, for example. If ever a man was, metaphorically speaking, drifting slowly and unable to make water it was he. There he was, counting his assets and congratulating himself on how well he'd screwed the Inland Revenue, when down they came like a wolf on the fold and soaked him for everything he'd got. All those years of fiddling while the tapes burned – wiped out in one terse final demand. Going to Pompidou's funeral must have seemed like more fun than he'd had in months. And what consolation could he find in the thought that even were he to make water there would certainly be a tax man lurking about demanding that he account for it?

Hard-hearted indeed is he who can consider the President's dilemma without wiping away a furtive grin. But let us not dwell on the subject for there is another far more deserving of our sympathy, name Henry Kissinger.

For ages now men have watched the progress of this improbable Casanova with admiration and awe, to say nothing of downright envy. How, we asked ourselves, did he manage it – this fat little chap, continually flitting hither and yon and always returning to the warm and eager embrace of some of the world's most desirable crumpet?

When finally middle-age began to take its toll, the nifty footwork (the bachelor's version of the Ali Shuffle) failed him, the razor-sharp reflexes lost their edge and, finding himself trapped in a corner and taking punishment, he succumbed to wedlock we all felt somehow that justice had been done.

It seemed only fair, after all. He'd had his share, by Heaven he had. It could even be argued that he'd had ours, too. But Oh! what a fall was there, my countrymen, for barely a week into his honey-moon the news has leaked out – Mrs Kissinger has made him stop biting his nails.

A small enough sacrifice, you might think. Biting your fingernails (and one assumes it's his fingernails he's promised to stop biting and not his toenails) may be a more convenient hobby than, say, building ships in bottles but it's not all that wildly enjoyable.

Nevertheless, it can only be regarded as ominous when a wife has got around to this kind of detail while still on honeymoon. It's woman's notorious reforming instinct that makes her take a small, stout, globe-trotting, nail-biting bachelor and try to turn him into something else. Reasonable enough, no doubt, to suppose that she's already made him promise to stop going out with girls.

That probably happened as he slipped the wedding ring on to her finger and hardly can his system have recovered from the shock when she was off on this new tack . . .

"Oh, and another thing, Henry."

"Vot, *mein* dollink?"

"Take your finger out of your mouth when you're talking to me, Henry. This nail biting has got to stop."

"But, *Himmel*, der other girls . . ."

"Don't mention those other girls to me, Henry. That's all over now, do you understand? Finished, kaput. And so is the nail biting, Henry. Nail biting may have been all right for those other girls. *Anything* may have been all right for those other girls. My goodness me, I never could see what you saw in *them* but I'm telling you, Henry – Henry, take your thumb out of your mouth this instant –

133

you're going to have to use a little willpower here or I may just send you off to see that nice President Sadat with bitter aloes all over your fingernails and you wouldn't like that would you, Henry dear?"

"Ach, no, *mein* dollink."

"That's right, Henry, and while we're about it, Henry– Henry! I caught you there, didn't I? You were just going to nibble your pinky, weren't you? – while we're about it, Henry, I'm not too happy with your figure. We're going to have to put you on a little diet, so just lay aside that Danish pastry and . . . Fingers, Henry, fingers!"

And so it goes on. As on the *Q.E.2*, so on the ship of matrimony – drifting slowly and unable to make water. Still, I don't suppose we have to tell Henry that. He must be finding it out already.

April 8, 1974

Passed Buck

The Queen's Palace servants, who, hitherto, have had to negotiate on pay and conditions through the Department of Employment, have won the right to make direct representations . . .

"Mrs B., thank goodness! I thought you weren't coming. You've no idea how relieved I was to see you trudging up the Mall."

"Oh, yer? Nearly didn't come at all, did I? Not after yesterday."

"Yesterday? Oh, dear, what happened yesterday?"

"You may well ask, duckie. All right for you, wasn't it? gallivantin' off with *'im* to open them there 'Ouses of Parliament. Dolled up like Lady Muck. I seen you– on the telly. I said to Alf, I said, 'There she goes, Alf, another new frock and all. All very well for some,' I said. Never left the key under the mat, though, did you? Had to climb through the scullery window, didn't I? Me – with my awful bronichals and all."

"Mrs B., I don't know what to say! I didn't know you had bronichals. And as for the key, well, I'm sure I asked Phil . . ."

"*'Im?* Fat lot *'e* cares! Wouldn't soil his hands *'e* wouldn't, putting the key under the mat. Which reminds me – how long's *'e* going to keep them polo ponies in the spare bedroom?"

"I really don't know, Mrs B. Oh dear, I'm not used to this sort of thing. Hadn't you better have a chat with the little man from the Department of Employment?"

"No good dragging him into it, duckie. Them days is over. Direct negotiations we have now, says so in the paper. No more messing about with toffee-nosed gits from the Department of Employment . . . Get me slippers out, there's a love."

"Slippers? Yes, of course. Er, where do you keep them?"

135

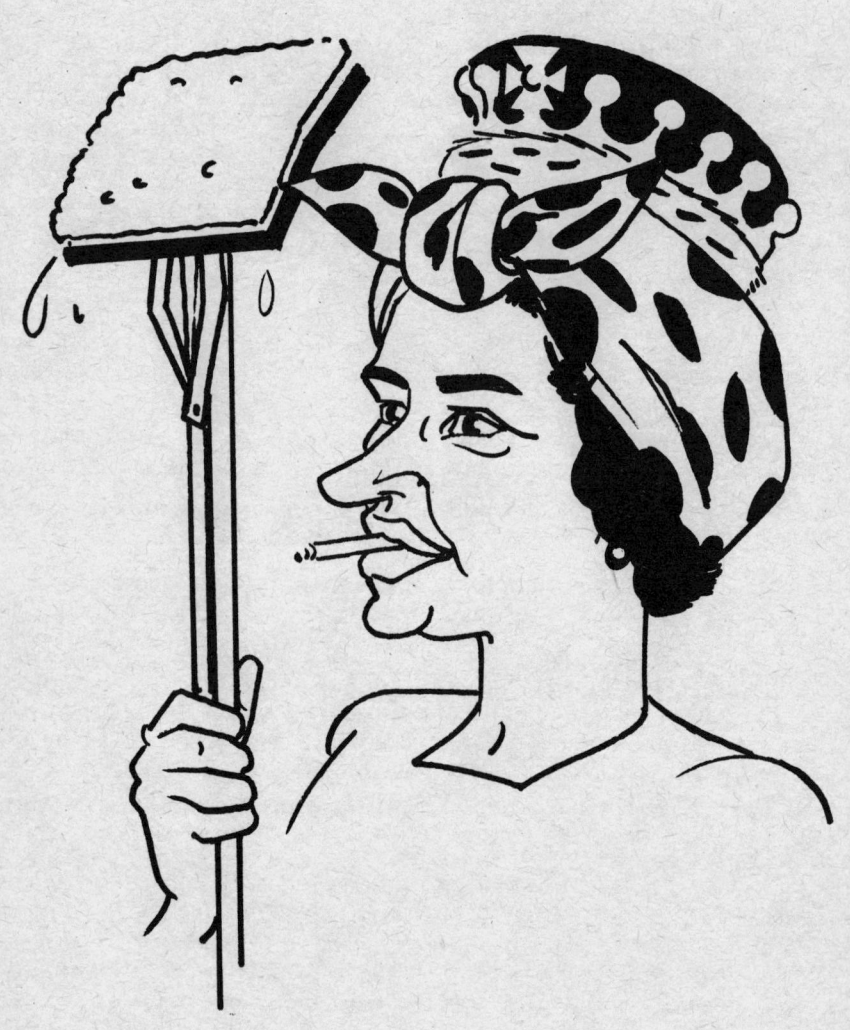

"In the broom cupboard, where do you think? No, not there – that's the bloody fridge, isn't it? Gawd strewf, doesn't even know where her own broom cupboard is, wouldn't credit it would you? . . . 'Ere, what about that list I left for you – did you get me lavender floor polish?"

"Well, no, I'm afraid not. I was going to ask the little man from the Department of . . ."

"Look, I've told you, we don't muck about with him no more. When I'm low on floor polish I come straight to you now, dearie. And another thing – I don't want all them Corgis yapping about when I'm down on my hands and knees in future. One of them bit my bum something cruel the other day and it's no good you telling me to take my bum up with the Department of Employment. From now on I take it up with you."

"I do apologise, Mrs B. I can't understand it. They've never bitten any of us on the . . . er . . ."

"Wouldn't hardly get the chance, would they? How often do they see you down on your hands and knees scrubbing floors? I want them Corgis locked up and I want them polo ponies out, too. All that dung all over the place, chokes up the Hoover something terrible, it does."

"Well, it's only till the new stables are ready and . . . Oh, very well. I'll have a word with Phil. He's busy at the moment but . . ."

"Busy? '*Im*? Oh, yes, I'm sure! When did '*e* last do a hand's turn? You should hear what my Alf has to say about '*im*, you really should, and by the way, if you hear a knock on the back door it'll be my Alf coming up to have a word with '*im*."

"Oh, dear. Phil hasn't upset your Alf, has he?"

"Upset him? I should say so? The times my Alf's complained about not having petrol for that motor mower . . . well, you wouldn't believe! Mentioned it times without number, he has, but does '*e* take any notice, oh no! Just walks up and down the garden path, '*e* does, with his hands behind his back. Wouldn't hurt '*im*, would it? to do a bit of weeding now and then, 'stead of leaving it all to my Alf, him being on penicillian and all. But oh, no, not old Lord High and bloody Mighty! Still, my Alf can tell '*im* straight now, can't he? what with direct negotiations. Much cosier, that is."

"Yes, Er, if you'll excuse me, Mrs B, I think I'll just go and lie down . . ."

"Ah, feeling poorly, are you? Bronichals I expect, same as me. Well, you just . . . Hang about! Cor blimey, haven't you got the bleeding kettle on yet? You know I can't do a stroke till I've had a nice cup of tea . . ."

May 27, 1974

137

We were heading for Dieppe and the Channel ferry and home and she said, "Where exactly are we then?"

I consulted a passing signpost. "Deville," I said.

"Doesn't seem much of a place, Deville," she said.

"True," I said, for on cursory examination it looked like the Gallic sister suburb of Cricklewood or Kilburn High Street without the Irish. "But on the other hand better the Deville you know than the Deville you . . ."

Her lips tightened a bit and she fell into a moody silence. She hadn't entirely recovered from an incident the previous day when we were driving northwards from Catalonia, land of such traditional Spanish delicacies as *paella* and squid and rape *mariniere* and chicken and chips, as well as more exotic dishes like prawn cocktail, lamb chops, great mixed grill meat, baked turbo and something which I never actually tasted but which, with admirable simplicity though a certain amount of ambiguity, was briefly called "baked".

Anyway, we were going through Correze and she said, "What's this next town we're coming to?"

"Well," I said, not wishing to spoil it, "it's about halfway between Cahors and Limoges."

"Are you sure?" she said. She'd lost a little faith in my map reading since the journey down when I'd taken us on an exhaustive, though impromptu, tour of Toulouse, insisting the whole time that the A.A. had got all the street names wrong.

I crossed my heart solemnly. "As I live and Brive," I said.

Well, you have to think of something to pass the time when you're sitting in the front passenger seat for 750 miles and irritating other people is as satisfying a hobby as any. Besides, I'd already exhausted such fun as was to be derived from trying to mislead the driver with such remarks as, "I'm not sure we can be on the right road. This one only leads to *Toutes Directions*."

However, I'm not exactly a bad passenger: I'm just a bored passenger. Apart from leaning over the seat every now and then to beat up the kids there's not a great deal to relieve the monotony when you're riding shotgun in a modern car.

"Why don't you look out of the window instead of sitting there moaning?" she asks, irritably. "Look at the countryside. For heaven's sake, it's not every day we drive through France."

Quite true, no doubt, and actually I'm very fond of the countryside but not when it's going by at a totally illegal eighty miles an hour. I always seem to miss the best bits.

"Oh, did you see *that!*" she says, moving out to pass a camion or two.

"What?" I say. "Where? Where?"

"That château behind the trees – twelfth century at the latest," she says. "Just over there."

"Don't look back!" I scream. "Don't look back!" In any case it's too late. All I can see by now is a billboard gloomily advocating the *repression de l'ivresse publique* or something just as socially conscious, although the sight of a bit of *ivresse publique* would cheer me up no end.

You may wonder why it is that I do ride shotgun on these excursions and the fact is that I don't like driving. We established this some years ago, about the time Cliff Michelmore presented one of those irritating TV quizzes to find out how well you can drive and she scored more points than I did.

"Well, that settles it," she said. "I'm clearly a better driver than you are so I'd better drive from now on. Anyway, you don't like driving, do you?" It was the first I'd heard of it but by that time I was too broken in spirit to argue and now it's too late.

There are occasions when I wouldn't mind taking the wheel but I hardly like to mention it these days. It would only cause bickering and ill-feeling and it could even mean that not only the holiday but the entire marriage simply went to rack and Rouen.

July 8, 1974

Claus and Effect

"Hang about," I said, casting my eyes through the list of peremptory Christmas demands, "who's this fellow Saunta Class, then?"

"Oh, you know," she said, irritably. She wasn't much interested because she was studying the lesson she had to read at the school carol service. I don't know what they teach them at primary schools these days, but it certainly isn't spelling. I mean, here she is pushing eleven and still writing about Saunta Class. What's more, she hasn't believed in him for ages. She just invokes his name around this time of year in the hope of striking a sentimental chord in the paternal heart. (Her sister does the same but when the top item on the Yuletide list is A PONY in block capitals, heavily underlined, it's amazing how unsentimental I can be.)

"Look," I said, "it's not a bad anagram except that you've been a bit generous with the esses. But you don't actually . . ."

She swept away, waving the New Testament about rather ostentatiously, and gave me that cool, contemptuous look she learnt from her mother. There's no such thing as a little girl, you know – they're all simply cut down women, from the day they're born.

Still, it was odd that Saunta Class should have cropped up just then because I'd seen him in London only an hour or so earlier. About five feet one he was, with his beard under his left ear, and he was handing out advertising pamphlets in the street. I would have approached him, murmuring words of Christmas cheer but there

139

was a look about him which suggested that the next person who said, "Ho, ho, ho" in his vicinity would get a festive knee in the groin.

I wasn't surprised, really. Poor old Saunta has been taking a considerable bashing lately. In our village his reputation has never quite recovered from the time he was impersonated at the Christmas bazaar by my friend Harry, a perfectly admirable Saunta Class in every respect save that he couldn't face the prospect of all those grasping kids without a few jars inside him, so that by the time he got out of the pub his breath was about 100 proof and all the little children reeled away from the Toyland Grotto stoned out of their tiny minds.

Well, I suppose that's roughly par for the course at a village bazaar but recently there's been a more organised and sinister campaign against the old chap. It originated, naturally, in America where he was attacked by the Health Institute who said he was overweight; by the American Fund for Animals because he kept cracking his whip over those reindeer; by the Black Power movement who complained that he was always depicted as white; and by Women's Lib who accused him of being a male chauvinist pig. A male chauvinist pig – him, the legendary benefactor of virgins!

All that and now this haphazard Saunta Class in my own home. The time had come, I thought, to strike a blow or two in the old boy's defence, especially as I remembered reading some background information about him only the other day. "Where", I said, as the typewriter warmed up, "are the colour supplements? I can't find them anywhere."

"Have you looked in the guinea pig's cage?" said my wife. I heaved an impatient sigh, for we've been this route before.

"Listen," I said, "you know perfectly well the guinea pig never takes the colour supplements. She doesn't like them. She's a *Guardian* reader. *The Guardian* makes a better nest than the colour supplements." (Actually, she'll take *The Times* if there's no *Guardian* available but I think that's mostly for the crossword puzzle.)

The point was, however, that there was no sign of the colour supplements and without the information they contained how could I write my classic piece beginning "Yes, there *is* a Saunta Class, Veronica" or whatever the kid was called in the famous American editorial? I searched through other publications in the hope of finding up-to-date intelligence of him (he got himself arrested in Oxford Street a couple of years ago, I remember) only to discover that my self-appointed task was unnecessary.

For there, in a Home Counties newspaper, was an advertisement from a department store offering not only the presence of Saunta Class himself *and* a toy for each child but Green Shield stamps as well. A Saunta hip enough to work himself in on the Green Shield stamps lark clearly needs no help from me. And if he happens to be slim, black, female and riding a bike too I think we can assume his future is assured.

December 23, 1974

Towel Play

Quite the nicest image of last week, conjured up after a report by the International Labour Organisation, was that of the domestic bliss in the home of Lord Elwyn Jones, the Lord Chancellor – he at the kitchen sink with a pinny over his robes and a mop in his hand, explaining patiently to his wife that his job would be a lot easier if she didn't let the fat congeal in the frying-pan; and she, I expect, darning busily away at the Woolsack and murmuring: "Sorry, dear. Try not to get the Fairy Liquid all over your wig. It makes you look such a fright when you go out in the rain."

All this emerged, of course, when the I.L.O. issued its report calling on men to share the burdens of housework – a call that was quite unnecessary in the home of the Lord Chancellor for, as his wife revealed, "he's an absolute darling about the house".

Well, if it comes to that I'm an absolute darling about the house, too, and so, I gather, is Stratford Johns. Michael Parkinson isn't. Michael Parkinson is a male chauvinist pig who believes in letting his wife do all the chores.

But I have to admit that the thing about us absolute darlings – or, at least, some of us absolute darlings since I can't speak for the Lord Chancellor or Mr Johns – is that we end up as absolute darlings because we have very little choice in the matter, although there are aspects of housework which I, for instance, refuse to take any part in; I mean the traditional farce of cleaning up the mess that we employ the cleaning lady to come in and clean up.

"Good Lord," says my wife, surveying the room and doing the thunderstruck bit. "Hasn't anybody cleaned up this mess?" Since she's just got back from taking the children to school and I'm the only one in the house, "anybody" seems an unnecessarily vague term, but I let it pass.

"It's all right," I say, "Shirley's coming in to clean up."

"Exactly," she says, beating hell out of cushions and taking away my coffee. "I can't ask Shirley to come in and clean up a mess like this."

At this point I do my impression of a journalist, make an excuse and leave. But it's in the matter of washing up that I'm forced into the role of absolute darling. "I can leave the washing-up to you, can't I?" she says, and vanishes for about three hours. God knows where she goes.

Now occasionally I try to beat the system. Not being a total fool I

141

don't actually refuse to do the washing-up, but I do it very badly. I leave the milk bottles on the draining-board. It drives her mad.

"You've left the milk bottles on the draining-board again," she says.

"I know," I say. "I like milk bottles on the draining-board. It gives the place a homely touch." She takes them away in a marked manner, bides her time and wreaks a terrible revenge. She waits till I'm sitting down to watch something important on the telly – an interview with the Prime Minister perhaps, the football results, or a film I've been trying to catch up with for ages – and then she brings the Hoover out.

"You don't mind if I just do a quick Hoover, do you?" she says. Brrrmmm.

"Yes, I do mind."

"Pardon?"

"I said, 'Yes, I do bloody mind.'"

"Sorry, can't hear you."

"Well, turn the bloody Hoover off then!"

"What? I can't hear you because of the Hoover, you see."

And so it goes on, and in the background Harold is puffing his pipe and mouthing away and not so much as an "ayoop" or a "sithee" gets through to me. By the time she switches the Hoover off, all that's left on the box is the menacing glare of Robin Day's glasses as he says, "a grave message indeed from the Prime Minister"; or Frank Bough is saying, "and that shock result brings us to the end of the football results", and I'll have to wait till tomorrow to find out how many the Spurs lost by this time; or the end credits are just coming on and I'm left shouting at the screen: "No, say that bit again – Rosebud was his *what?*"

And the next day when she says, "I can leave the washing-up to you, can't I?" I take the milk bottles outside and she thinks I'm an absolute darling, just like the Lord Chancellor.

January 13, 1975

Lust Orders

What happened was that I'd had lunch with these old friends, some of whom I hadn't seen for several days, and I got back a bit late. Well, it was half-past ten actually. Well, it might have been eleven. I say it was half-past ten but she says it was eleven and I can't really argue because I'd taken what my friend Wally calls "the pretty way home" and the clock was out of focus.

Naturally, I was prepared for the inevitable verbal onslaught and indeed I had the perfect answer. But I found her surprisingly, not to say ominously, calm. She waited till I'd completed my joyous reunion with various household animals and then she said, "I was hoping you'd be back earlier to drive me to the hospital and get my foot X-rayed."

Now I had noticed that she'd taken to walking with a rather unattractive limp but I hadn't liked to mention it for fear of making her self-conscious. Presently, however, she removed her shoe and revealed a swollen foot in disgusting shades of blue, black and brown.

"I dropped a 28-lb flower-pot on it," she said, modestly, "from about chest height. I think it's broken."

At this point, of course, I remembered my perfect answer to the expected remonstrations. "Ah," I said. "Yes. Well. That's what I wanted to tell you. I've not been out getting emotional for my own pleasure, you know. I did it for you. You see, there's this doctor writing in the *British Medical Journal* who says virtuous husbands are more of a mental strain to their wives than husbands who get drunk and gamble and lech after other women. The wives of virtuous husbands are all uptight and frustrated because they've nothing to complain about to their friends. And, well, it occurred to me that I'd been thoughtlessly virtuous for quite a long time and therefore the decent thing to do was to give you something to moan about."

She didn't say anything; too moved, I expect, by my consideration. But after a bit . . . "Have you been gambling and leching as well?" she said.

"No," I said. "I thought I'd do it by easy stages. Get drunk to start with and then move on to gambling and leching later." Obviously I hadn't begun a moment too soon. If she was already reduced to attention-seeking by dropping flower-pots on her feet she could easily end up doing herself a serious mischief.

Mind you, she can think herself lucky she's not married to a clergyman or a doctor. Apparently, they're much the worst offenders when it comes to being virtuous and leading their wives a terrible life. The offices of marriage-guidance councillors up and down the country at this very minute are probably full of these neurotic, broken-hearted wives sobbing out their pitiful tales . . .

"I tell you I don't know where to turn, really I don't. My husband . . . well, he's a beast – there's no other word for it. And since they made him a rural dean he's got worse.

"He never lays a hand on me, even in self-defence. Brings me a cup of tea in bed every morning, cooks the breakfast, gets the children off to school, helps with the washing-up and the house-work, doesn't smoke or drink . . . I don't think I can stand it a minute longer. I go round to my friends and they're all complaining away, happy as larks, and I haven't a thing to say.

"I thought, the other day, things were starting to get better. He came into breakfast with booze on his breath but it turned out he'd only been to Communion . . . My first husband, ah, now there was a lovely man. Stoned out of his mind, he was, from morning to night. Probably stoned all night as well for all I know but I never saw him then, of course. He was always out with his other women at night.

"Oh, he was a real smasher, he was. Gamble? My goodness, you've never seen anyone gamble like he did. Gambled away all his salary, his insurance policies, the furniture, the house . . . He died, though – drunk in bed with a girl he'd picked up for a bet. Saddest day of my life, that was. Well, no. I suppose the saddest day was when I married this swine I've got now . . ."

A survey carried out last week for a women's magazine revealed that one in four wives was unfaithful. No doubt they're the ones with virtuous husbands – driven into their lovers' arms through the sheer boredom of having nothing to natter about with the girls. The moral is clear for all us married chaps: it's our solemn duty, distasteful though it may be, to do our share of drinking, gambling and leching if only to keep the home together.

April 21, 1975

5

Unclassified Information

If you don't mind, I'd rather not discuss the morality of my having a holiday in Greece. I resolved it anyway with an English doctor with a pushchair whom I met on a hillside at Pelekas. He said he would have to search his conscience before buying a villa there and I said I should have to search mine too (to say nothing of my bank account) and we parted spiritually refreshed.

However . . .

"First," said the tour guide, beaming the beam he had learnt at tour guides' evening classes, "the bad news – your hotel's not built yet."

I never used to believe those stories about package-deal holidays. I thought the press made them up for a laugh: you know, lurid tales about lift shafts with no lifts and warning notices that you never saw till you fell on them from eighteen storeys up; lavatories that wouldn't flush unless you jumped up and down on the seat; sewage that came through the bath taps and beaches that were "100 yards from hotel", the rather important fact not being vouchsafed until too late that the 100 yards were straight down a close relative of the north face of the Eiger.

And yet here we were with nowhere to go except, apparently, a building-site. There was, of course, the usual chorus of outrage: ". . . strong letter of protest . . ." ". . . consult my solicitor . . ." ". . . crooked bastards . . ." – but in fact it turned out very well.

We had booked an inexpensive holiday in a second-class resort; we got instead, at no extra charge, two weeks in a luxury hotel with abundant and inventive meals and a genius who made such cakes as only a taste bud could find words to describe.

Naïvely he called these masterpieces "English cakes", which naturally prompted me to take the management on one side and make them swear on the Colonels' lives never to let him travel to England and discover the bitter truth.

All in all, therefore, you might think we had landed well but that would be to forget the overwhelming British need to suffer. This first manifested itself in complaints about the absence of film shows and the deplorable non-availability of a bingo caller.

Then, after a week, the tour guide came around to say that the original hotel was now completed and would we like to move there? One of our number had already been on a "recce" and reported that, thus far, the place consisted of a concrete slab in the middle of a dust bowl with only builders' rubble by way of adornment but, even so, well over half the party volunteered to go.

An Englishman who has paid for austerity is not going to be fobbed off with mere luxury or, as their spokesman put it, "I know it can't be half as good as this but I think we ought to try it." There was a dogged look in his eyes and a rigidity about his upper lip and he would have acquitted himself well in the Blitz.

We, the sybarites who remained, saw the others off in their coach. They smiled bravely and waved and, though they didn't actually sing "It's a long way to Tipperary", I expect they would have done if they'd thought of it.

The next time they appeared was when we were waiting for the plane home. They shuffled into the airport lounge, sort of furtively but with a kind of bewildered relief as if they had suddenly been granted amnesty after serving half their sentence. They looked paler than the rest of us, too, as though the sun hadn't bothered to shine much on their part of the island.

"How'd it go?" I inquired of one of them. He had a weary droop to his mouth and lines of strain across his forehead.

"Well," he said, "the beach was a fair walk and there was a beat group that played all night so you couldn't sleep a lot and they gave us ham and chips for lunch."

I, who had stepped straight from the hotel on to the best beach on the island, who had mercifully not heard a beat group in weeks, and who had lunched daily on such snacks as dolmades, kebabs, moussaka, and strawberries soaked in maraschino, was about to offer words of condolence when he sighed mournfully and said: "It was just the sort of holiday I'd been looking forward to. How was yours?"

"Oh," I said. "You know. Not bad." There was no point in discussing it further because my holiday had quite clearly lacked the one vital ingredient that his had contained: I had absolutely nothing to moan about.

May 29, 1972

Vot a Carry Off

There was this irate Londoner in the middle of the road watching a taxi snatched from under his nose for the umpteenth time in half an hour and as the blue-rinsed occupants flashed their well-kept, infuriating teeth at him his self-control snapped. "Bloody tourists!" he yelled.

Had Sir Geoffrey de Freitas (Lab., Kettering), been around he might well have sympathised. "When I have great difficulty in crossing the road to get to this House because of swarms of tourists," said Sir Geoffrey, the other day, "I feel that enough is enough and that this corner of the island is beginning to sink under the weight of visitors."

Quite right. Tourists, if you'll pardon the phrase, are a pain in the ass. The English-speaking ones are intolerable enough because they grab all the taxis, the best cinema and theatre seats and the last table in every restaurant and waste your time asking damn fool questions

148

that you can't answer – like who built the National Gallery.

But even worse are the ones who speak no English and, possessing neither guide nor phrase-book, attempt to communicate by telepathy.

"Look, if yer can't speak bloody English, I can't bloody 'elp yer, can I?" said the bus conductor, exasperated to a point where his traditional bus conductor's courtesy had quite deserted him.

The couple thus addressed, tiny, elderly and born losers, smiled and nodded at him in that aggravatingly humble and patient way that uni-lingual tourists have.

Naturally I kept my head down and carried on reading John Arlott. But, alas, my wife who, in an earlier age and a different station in life, would have been observed in country lanes, taking gruel to the sick, said, "Oh, poor things", and within seconds we were lumbered.

"*Parlez-vous français? Italiano? Deutsch?*" No, of course they didn't. They *parlez-voused* nothing except some foul, guttural tongue of their very own. And they smiled and nodded and showed us a card with an address in Oxford Street and the man closed his eyes and laid his cheek on his hands and for a moment of indignation I thought he was asking my wife to sleep with him.

"Oh, look," said my wife, who speaks telepathy rather well, "they want an hotel." So we dragged them up Oxford Street to this address and it turned out to be a camera shop.

"They can't live in a camera shop," I said. But I pointed it out to the man who smiled and nodded and was touched at my kindness in bringing this sight to his attention, though clearly puzzled as to why I should have imagined he would be interested in a camera shop.

He then turned his card over and, for the first time, revealed an address on the other side – the address of an hotel, simply miles away – and went through his going to sleep routine again.

"Why didn't you show me this in the first place, you old fool?" I said. And he smiled and nodded and his wife smiled and nodded and I felt like punching both of them.

So then we had to find them a taxi and, of course, we couldn't because the taxis were full of other rotten tourists, all beaming at us through the windows like the Queen Mother.

"What shall we do?" said my wife.

"Push them under a bus and run," I said. We were already late for lunch.

"No, no," she said. "Shall we give them some money?"

"What on earth for?" I said. "They ought to be giving us money." Well, after all, bunging them would have defeated the whole object. Why do we have tourists here if it isn't to take them for every penny they've got and so help to balance the national budget and keep old Ted afloat?

Anyway, a cab drew up eventually and disgorged a load of Elmers and Homers and Betty-Anns and Mary-Lous and we bundled our lot in and gave instructions to the driver and they shook our hands and smiled and nodded and I felt like the wedding guest when he finally got shot of the Ancient Mariner.

In 1971, according to Mr Anthony Grant (Under-Secretary, Industrial Development) Britain earnt £500 millions from overseas visitors and, if my experience is anything to go by, earnt is the right word. All I got from playing a reluctant Good Samaritan was a nagging sense of worry that perhaps something dreadful had happened to those helpless, hopeless people as soon as they were out of my sight. Bloody tourists.

August 14, 1972

Road Ode

The people of Grantchester (where, as Rupert Brooke reminds us, "their skins are white; they bathe by day, they bathe by night") are worried about a proposed by-pass that could play havoc with their slumbrous streams and bosky woods.

These developments may be vague at the moment, but, since they include a possible relief road from Trumpington to Grantchester meadows, the fears are not entirely groundless.

Grantchester folks – straight-eyed men and women who love the Good and worship Truth and laugh uproariously in youth, when not begetting lithe children lovelier than a dream – obviously don't want to be connected in any way with Trumpington where, as is well known, they throw worse than oaths at one.

Besides, a damn great by-pass trundling round the place would make poor Rupert's loving and nostalgic little poem, to say nothing of Grantchester itself, look pretty sick. The whole thing would have to be rewritten, a task which, Brooke fans will be relieved to learn, I have already undertaken.

> *And in that garden, by arc light,*
> *Men build motorways all night;*
> *And spectral clump before the dawn,*
> *A hundred Navvies down the lawn;*
> *And oft, where once were boughs, is seen*
> *The shade of a cement machine.*

I thought I'd leave the following stuff about Ditton girls being mean and dirty. I've never met any Ditton girls, but if Brooke says they're mean and dirty, that's good enough for me. On, then, to the next relevant passage. Thus:

Ah, God! to see great road drills stir
Across the fields at Grantchester!
To smell the choking-sweet and rotten
Unforgettable, unforgotten
Diesel fumes, and hear the spades
Digging up the leafy glades.
Say, do the Wimpey men still stand
With those of Cubitt, Laing and Shand?

It all adds, I fancy, an abrasive touch of realism to Brooke's homesick and, let's face it, jingoistic yearnings. Even Grantchester must come to grips with the 1970s and realise there's no place any more for trout streams and fauns a-peeping through the green.

Oh! Yet stands the Church clock at ten to three?
And has the whistle blown for tea?

April 28, 1972

Ava Gonow and Co

The last letter I received from Bernard Levin (a young journalist on whose stumbling progress I keep a fatherly eye and whose head I tend to pat encouragingly from time to time) ran as follows: "Have we had that Swedish assassin Dag Ersdrorn?"

Upon reading it I uttered a tortured cry and, in a hand trembling much as his had done, I immediately scribbled my response: "No, and I don't think we've had the Russian spin-bowler Lev Tarmova, either." By then I knew that the damage was done and there was no turning back – the fever was upon us.

This is a game that has, in its time, driven us both to the very brink of insanity, the symptoms of its insidious grip being glazed, unseeing eyes, mumbling lips and the murmuring of strange incantations. "Helen Highwater," the sufferer mutters, sometimes to perfect strangers, "Jerry Attrix . . . Aidan D'Abett . . . Pugh Bickair . . ."

We were introduced to it, Levin and I, by one Julian Holland, who now masquerades as an editor on *The World at One*, when we all worked together in the same office and, being unable to find anything better to do, were desperate for kicks. It was this Holland who, one day, mentioned a mythical American called Phil D. Basket who used to exhort New Yorkers to throw their litter into bins rather than the street, and at once we were hooked.

From Phil D. Basket it was but a short step to Mahatma Kote, the Indian cloakroom attendant, Segovia Karpett, the drunken musician and Mustapha Phix, the Turkish drug addict; while pretty soon we realised that if Warren Peace was the biographer of Tolstoy, then Bertha D. Blews must be a jazz singer, just as Rudy Day was a regretful husband and Lotty Cairs his neglected wife.

Very swiftly this became known as "the Phil D. Basket game" and nobody got any work done at all. Men would sit up far into the night reading dictionaries for inspiration and come in the next day, red-eyed but triumphant, shouting, "What about Bosun Arrows, the nautical archer, and Walter Wall, the carpet salesman, and Jonah Farck, the transvestite saint, and Stan Dandyliver, the highwayman, and . . ."

Oh, quite, quite. And what about Fay Slifter, the plastic surgeon, and Gloria Stevvon, the West Country beauty queen, and Sailor Vee, the easy-going seafarer? Oh, there was no end to them.

After a bit other addicts joined in, too. Kenneth Tynan produced the French waltz expert, Charles Louis D'Ince, and Benny Green the untidy Asian, Ram Shackel, and Ronnie Scott (the jazz club man) introduced Xavier Breth, the flamenco dancer.

Then our lives (not to mention our poor, crazed minds) became crowded with some very strange people indeed, many of them foreign – a Dutch folksinger called Hans Neezen-Boomzerdayzee, a dance hall cleaner named Artur di Ballwass-Ova, various Chinese such as Chou-en-Gum and Tai Pist (a drunken stenographer, presumably). Ann Tzinner-Pantz, the Middle European contortionist, and Beau Neidel, the lazy German fop.

And, too, there were Yul Brynner's cousin, Baldur Zerkoot, and Art Sidewright, the international footballer, and Celia Lipps, the spy mistress, to say nothing of Belle Tupp, the professional heckler, Shaw Tandwrighter, the Clerk of the court and TV pundits like Mark Mywerdz and Liz N. Toomie and such alcoholics as Totus Attick and Les Avanuther.

I could go on pretty well indefinitely. At the last approximate count we had assembled a cast of well over 300 people, all of them closely related to Phil D. Basket. But, of course, the truly mind-blowing thing, and the reason why, once hooked, you can never kick the habit, is that the list is inexhaustible.

The Brendan Behan play, *Richard's Cork Leg*, produced one addition – an Irish tart called Crystal Clear (employed, I expect, by my favourite madame, E. C. Vertue), although what she proves really is that, in the Phil D. Basket business Behan was only an amateur.

But best of all – a perfect example of life giving art a thrashing at its own game – was the news the other day that the runner-up in the world speedway championships was a Swede called Bernt Persson. To be called Bernt Persson and deliberately to become a speedway rider seems like a wilful challenge to the gods and one can only keep one's fingers crossed for him. Nevertheless, Bernt Persson is surely as clear a winner of the Phil D. Basket Gold Medal as Hans Downe or Art Wright, unless, of course, someone produces a genuine Norwegian bartender named Lars Torders.

September 25, 1972

'Roo the Day

Now that Australia has decided to abandon "God Save the Queen" and adopt a national anthem of its own, all-comers being welcome to put forward suggestions, a splendid opportunity has arisen for an ambitious songwriter to find his niche in history.

The reward for the winning composition – to be chosen by popular acclaim – will be £3,000, so clearly the competition is going to be stiff. Over the next three months, no doubt, it will be almost impossible to camp beside a billabong or wait under a coolibah tree till your billy boils without being disturbed by an eager swagman with furrowed brow and pencil gripped in both hands as he composes some such stirring and patriotic sentiment as, for instance:

> *Austral-yer! Austral-yer!*
> *We'll never let yer down or fail-yer.*

Nevertheless, and undeterred, I entend to go ahead with my own offering and perhaps it's only fair, in the circumstances, to warn all other contenders now that they are wasting their energies and would be better off chasing wallabies up blue-gum trees or whatever Australians do to pass the idle hours.

Of course, and I make this clear in my own defence, I am not, myself, an Australian. Indeed, I can say without a twinge of remorse, that I have never ever been there but I don't regard either of these things as a handicap.

In this matter of composing national anthems, the trick is to place your finger firmly on the country's pulse, to capture its very flavour. So the first consideration in an Australian anthem is to reflect the richness of the vocabulary and the curious nomenclature of the citizenry, as well as the image projected in the advertising campaigns of a land of space and plenty and leisure and easy living.

Therefore, my anthem, sung roughly to the tune of "Land of Hope and Glory", begins like this:

> *Come now, Cobber and Digger,*
> *Darlene, Charlene and Blue,*
> *Let's all sing out "Fair dinkum!",*
> *"You beaut!" and "Stone the crows!" too.*

For this land of Australia,
full of outback and sheep,
Where there's nothing to do
but fall down dead drunk asleep.

Naturally, it's a little rough at the moment but I flatter myself I'm on the right lines there. On hearing those words sung, I venture to suggest that even the hardest-bitten Australian would find it difficult to suppress the odd sentimental tear as he downed his eighteenth schooner of lager.

So, having got the first verse more or less settled, we come to the problem of what to put in the second and here, I think, one ought to pay tribute to Australia's need for more population, its renowned hospitality and the adventurousness and wanderlust of its inhabitants. Thus:

Welcome Wops and Limeys,
   Frogs and Heinies, too.
You'll all make good Australians,
   if crossed with a kangaroo.
In an ice-cold Fosters,
   toast the land of the free —
You can keep Australia,
   it's off to Europe for me.

At this point, it seems to me, one should bear in mind that Australia is a young country and still a fairly remote one and that many people in other lands know little of it, except that its aristocracy are all descended from convicted felons; that its beaches are littered the whole year round with huge sun-dazed girls called Sheila; and that the streets of its cities are full of men who not only have the exclusive rights to the freehold of Sydney bridge but are prepared to sell them to the first foreigner they meet for several thousand pounds or the price of a drink, which ever is the more convenient.

The rest, I am confident, will come to me in time. After all, I have three months in which to apply the final polish and if the Australian Government cares to send me an advance on the £3,000, I shall devote myself to this most assiduously.

January 29, 1973

The bloke who commissioned me to put this book together has strong Australian connections. He would only allow the inclusion of this piece if his printable comments on it were made known: "A lot of old cobbers . . . wouldn't give you three quid for the anthem – with your Test team thrown in!"

This piece was prompted by the claim of Prof. A. L. Rouse that he had at last unravelled the identity of Shakespeare's "Dark Lady of the Sonnets".

Humour Roused

I wish to make it clear that this column, like any other bits and pieces I scribble from time to time in a desperate bid to earn a crust, is dedicated to Mr J. H. This information, of course, can be of little interest to my contemporaries and I only make it public now for the sake of posterity and future historians.

Four hundred years hence, when my collected works are on everybody's bookshelf, bitter controversy will doubtless rage as to the true identity of the author. Well, I don't mind that. I don't mind if one school of thought says that this column, like its fellows, was actually written by Alistair Cooke because he needed the money but was too ashamed to sign his name to such work.

Nor do I care if another school has it that the complete works of B. Norman were really produced in one hilarious evening by a consortium of three redundant and drunken sub-editors, the P.E. Instructor at Roedean, the ˙Master of Trinity and Miss Barbara Cartland.

For that matter it's of no importance to me even if someone tries to attribute authorship to Martin Bormann who was erroneously believed to have perished in a bunker in Berlin.

And I say this quite recklessly in the knowledge that now the idea has been suggested the *Daily Express* will second its gardening correspondent to follow me all over South America, should I ever go there, in a public-spirited, though misguided, attempt to bring me to justice.

That kind of stuff is of peripheral concern to us authors. As, too, are the Ph.D theses that will be written in centuries to come by earnest students trying to establish what the Great Man really meant when he wrote in February, 1972, that Mrs Margaret Thatcher was "kin to animals". (The fact that what the Great Man actually wrote was "kind to animals", only the "d" got left off in the excitement of the composing room, is neither here nor there. Let these potential Ph.D.s work it out for themselves.)

No, the only thing that really bothers me is the thought that future generations may, left to themselves, get my love life all wrong. I'm deeply afraid that 409 years after my birth some Oxbridge historian will publish a tome called, for the sake of argument, *Norman the Man*, in which he adduces that all my more lyrical passages were inspired by the fact that I was hopelessly, passionately, and irrevocably in love with, say Miss Glenda Jackson.

This he will surely prove, beyond question of doubt, by pointing out triumphantly that (a) not only did Miss Jackson and I live in or around London at precisely the same time but (b) she appeared in films and I was known to my friends and colleagues as a regular cinema-goer. To him that will provide incontrovertible evidence that she and I must certainly have met and equally certainly fallen in love.

And if that were not enough to convince the sceptics he will produce the hitherto undiscovered diary of some such popular astrologer of the time as, for example, the late Maurice Woodruff in which there appears the following entry: "June 6. Charity Ball at Dorchester, Read palms next to tombola stall. Much excitement when the famous writer Barry Norman gate-crashed, drunk, and was thrown out. No sign of Glenda Jackson."

In the hands of a skilled historian such mysterious and inconclusive words could be lethal. They could, apart from anything else, inspire people to reveal that the name "Glenda Jackson" can be found in everything I write if you take the second letter of the fourth word in the first paragraph and the first letter of the eighth word in the ninth paragraph and the fourth letter of the fifth word in the . . . well, you know.

Therefore, I wish everyone to be quite clear that all my work is dedicated not to Miss Jackson or any other lady, dark or fair (with the exception of my wife to whom, some years ago, I dedicated a novel that nobody wanted to publish) but to Mr J. H.

Some people, I suppose, will take this to mean I've joined the ranks of Gay Lib but, with due respect to Gay Lib, this is not so. Mr J. H. is my patron, just as the Earl of Southampton was Shakespeare's patron.

Mr J. H. is the man who, in return for the deeds of my house and all my insurance policies, will lend me the money to buy a new car. Mr J. H. is the man without whom I could not survive. Mr J. H. is, in short, my bank manager.

April 30, 1973

A Drop of Shivers Regal

Now that Princess Anne is to be married – to Mark Phillips if you believe her version, or the son of the Duke of Wellington if you place greater credence in *France-Dimanche* – it occurs to me that a lot of journalists are going to make a lot of money by writing their royal reminiscences.

Whenever a member of royalty gets mixed up in something juicy like marriage, magazine editors rush out into the highways and byways (to say nothing of the taverns and hostelries) of Fleet Street in search of professional Royal Family watchers who, for the price of a few rounds in El Vino's, will share with the reading public their most treasured memories of the member in question.

"My Life with Princess Anne"– that sort of stuff. I may say, with some degree of certainty, that none of them has actually lived with Princess Anne but you'll know what I mean.

The trick in writing royal reminiscences is not simply to stretch the available anecdotes as far as they will go but to give the impression that, for reasons of delicacy, you're concealing more than you can reveal since you are, of course, a gentleman whose lips are naturally sealed.

This is very gratifying to readers of such articles who like to believe, on the one hand, that all members of the Royal Family are of such purity and innocence that they wouldn't understand what Lord Lambton was doing even if provided with diagrams and the *News of the World*'s special offer, presentation album of happy snaps and, on the other, that they are nevertheless– and in their own regal and ermine-lined way– not without their own minor indiscretions.

Anyway, while musing thus the thought occurred to me that if royal reminiscences were the saleable commodity of the moment, why not sell mine? For I, too, have had my dealings with royalty. Oh, yes.

Prince Philip once shook his fist at me and that must be worth a bob or two somewhere, surely. Unfortunately, I can't for the life of me remember why. What could I have done to cause so regal and ducal a fist to be raised aloft and brandished in my direction?

The truth is, I think he did it because I was there. It was a long time ago in his less mellow days when he reacted to the word "journalist" like Pavlov's dogs to the dinner gong. A casual mention of it and his right fist shot out independently from behind his back and thumped the air.

Years later I met him again at a buffet lunch and he addressed me quite amiably. "Did you get enough to eat?" he asked.

"Yes, thanks," I said. "Did you?"

"Yes, thanks," he said, and I jotted the conversation down at once because, to a Royal Family watcher, an exchange of that calibre is worth at least 1,000 words and many guineas.

Unhappily, alas, it's not Prince Philip who's getting married but Princess Anne and with her I really blew my prospects. I dined with her once, you know, and at a party afterwards in my editor's office monopolised her for two hours.

Two hours! People have written three-part series about her on flimsier acquaintance. Where then is my three-part series? Where indeed. I have to confess to a total lack of recall of the entire occasion on account of the fact that I was quite drunk at the time.

I say this with chagrin and even shame. Not so long ago, after all, being drunk in charge of royalty would have entitled me to a permanent grace and favour residence in the Tower.

Royalty being more tolerant these days I was allowed to go home where I awoke the next morning as from a lost weekend and muttered into the phone: "I can't work today. I'm ill."

And my immediate superior, who had witnessed all, said bitterly, "Ill? I hope you bloody die."

What had I done? "Well," said the fashion editor, eyeing me strangely when next I appeared, "you weren't so much chatting to the Princess as chatting her up." Was that all? She wouldn't mind that, surely? The fashion editor laughed enigmatically and walked away.

I sent a note to the editor, the giver of the feast. "Dear Arthur," I wrote, trading in alcoholic remorse on past friendship, "thanks for the splendid party. It seems to have gone very well. Luv."

"Dear Norman," he wrote back. "I daresay in time the Princess will learn to forgive you. Yours faithfully." I've never been asked to meet royalty since. I don't know why. Anne, tell me, was it something I said?

June 11, 1973

Vital Statistic

Sir Geoffrey Howe, Minister for Trade and Consumer Affairs, was asked in the House the other day to set up an inquiry into the practice, adopted by some firms, of taking photographs of customers who pay for goods by cheque. Sir Geoffrey didn't think he'd bother. No point, really he said; it was only done in the case of people who had no acceptable means of identification.

I don't know what brought the question up but I imagine it had to do with the kind of photographs taken on the trading premises of such as Mr and Mrs Colin Levy. At first these were thought to have some sinister purpose but in view of recent developments it becomes clear that they are simply a normal business precaution.

What happened, no doubt, was that the customer paid by cheque in advance – as is, I believe, the practice in such establishments as Mrs Levy's where the principle of cash on delivery has never found much favour – and a few minutes later the lady said, "Oh, by the way, sir, do you have any acceptable means of identification?"

Well, by this time the customer had certainly taken off his jacket and very possibly his trousers, too, and naturally found himself in a rather difficult situation. Indeed, unless he belonged to one of those families in which it's well known that the eldest son always has a strawberry-shaped birthmark in a place not normally open to public inspection, it would be virtually impossible to prove his identity at all.

That being so, it would be only prudent of the Mr Levys to get out their cameras and take a few snaps because, even though the customer was ever so well-spoken and quite the gentleman, it's better to be safe than sorry, especially where cheques are concerned.

However, be that as it may. The thought that now occurs is, how *do* you prove your identity these days? No good leaving your name and address because businesses, banks and computers aren't interested in names and addresses – only in numbers.

If, for example, you happened to be a stout, silver-haired gentleman with a fixed grin who walked into a shop to buy a £45,000 yacht by cheque, saying, "My name's Edward Heath and I live at 10 Downing Street", the assistant would immediately reply, "Oh, yes? Do you have any acceptable means of identification?"

Whereupon, before he would accept your cheque and wrap the yacht, you would be obliged to prove that, whatever other pseudonym you masqueraded under, you were far more importantly the holder of, say, driving licence number 6A/43215 or V.A.T.-payer No. 874 2309 66.

Of course, once you'd identified yourself, the assistant would nip round to his mate at the back of the shop and show him your driving licence, saying, "Here, look who's just come in!"

"What? Not *the* 6A/43215?"

"The very same."

"Well, well. Good old 6A/4."

"Oh, giving ourselves airs, are we? When did he give you permission to call him by his first numbers?"

Because, you understand, that's what it'll come to eventually. One day we'll each be given an all-purpose number to last us through life and when it happens it'll be quite a relief. At present I sit at my desk, trying to work out who I am. And who I am is six figures, one letter and a stroke on a driving licence; twelve figures on a Barclaycard; ten on a telephone exchange; twelve figures, two letters and three strokes on an income tax assessment; eight figures on a bank account. Once I lived in a Hertfordshire village; now I live in SG36ST.

The more I think of it the more I realise the advantages of dispensing with confusing things like names and just having one comprehensive number. For a start, firms will no longer demand photographs of a customer with a dodgy cheque. They'll simply ask him to lower his trousers so that they can read the number tattoed from infancy across his buttocks.

"I baptise this child 876425390860097452183 . . ." And if the kid doesn't like his number, so what? He can always get it changed by Deed Poll.

July 2, 1973

Fighting on the Beaches

It was about dawn when the noise woke me, the sullen noise of a plane, full-laden and heavy, bearing its deadly cargo towards some distant target. My wife stirred uneasily. "It's all right," I said. "It's one of ours."

I stood on the lawn in my pyjamas, waving as the plane went by, and there was a patriotic lump in my throat, an emotional tear in my eye. "Our boys," I murmured. "Our gallant lads." And I offered up a silent prayer for them and for our gallant girls and gallant children, too.

The aircraft droned on out of sight. It was only, I knew, the first of the day, the pathfinder. Even now others just like it were lining up at airfields all over the country, ready to launch another series of non-stop daylight raids on Europe.

How many of their occupants, I wondered, would return unscathed? And even as that anxious thought passed through my mind the night raiders were coming home, touching down after their midnight flights from Malaga, Bilbao, San Remo, Nice and Torremolinos.

I thought of them stumbling out of their planes, shattered and exhausted and clutching the souvenirs of their campaign, the pathetic little mementos collected by every such expeditionary force . . .

A bit of mock-Toledo gold here, a litre of plonk there and (with memories of a sacrifying article in a Sunday newspaper) a dose of clap over there. And probably over there, too, and over there as well, I shouldn't wonder.

I imagined them at the debriefing, huddled around their kit in the chill grey of early morning, as their hoarse, dry-lipped leader spoke for them all . . .

"Well, we did all right at first. Got right down to the beaches of the Costa Brava. The local people seemed friendly, even glad to see us. But I remember, I turned to Fred here and I said, 'It's quiet Fred – too quiet. I don't like it.'

"But Fred just laughed because, well, it looked like it was going to be a doddle. They had, you know, all the signs up – 'Tea Like Mother Makes', 'Chips With Everything', 'English Speaked Here' – and we were pretty well-equipped. Or so we thought. But . . ." He ran a trembling hand over his brow down which the cold sweat trickled. His gaze was turned inwards on memories almost too painful to talk about. "What we didn't know was that Jerry was ready for us.

"He waited, Jerry, till we'd established a beachhead – and then he struck. It was a massacre. I've never seen anything like it. Just bombarded the place with Deutschmarks, he did, poured them in like there was no tomorrow. Even the Yanks retreated. The dollar itself couldn't stand up to Jerry.

"As for us, well, what could our poor little lightweight pounds do against the mighty mark? We fought, of course, to the last shilling. But from the moment that first Panzer division arrived, we knew we'd had it. We lost the beach mats first, then the deck chairs, then the best tables in the restaurants. Jerry took 'em all. We tried – God knows we did. And the pound kept floating; it was too weak to sink.

"But the crunch came when even the peseta turned against us. We knew all along we couldn't compete with the franc or the lira but at least we'd thought we could hold our own with the bloody peseta. But, no – it was stronger than we suspected. We were outgunned, surrounded. In the finish we just managed to get back aboard the planes and beat it for home."

There was stark horror in the speaker's eyes. "I never want to live through anything like that again."

The coaches and cars arrived to take the survivors back to their home bases, there to begin the slow, painful process of healing their shattered wallets and deeply wounded pockets. Once I'd have been among them but I was in a raid on Europe last year and I saw, even then, the way the battle was going.

So this time when they called for volunteers and the reckless and foolhardy scrambled aboard the planes I looked the other way. I stayed here, in the Home Guard, defending Britain's beaches against the foreign invader. Call me a coward if you will – but after two weeks' service on the Devon coast I'm here to say that I didn't exactly come out of it unscarred either. The pound's putting up a pretty lousy fight in this country, too, you know.

August 20, 1973

Meet a Maid

I can't really claim to have had much intercourse with traffic wardens, apart from shouting "*Heil* Hitler" whenever I pass one.

Perhaps it's an illusion created by the dreaded uniform but they seem to have the ability to see right through you; to look you over with the cold, unblinking stare that's issued along with the cap badge and know at once that, however convincingly you masquerade as an innocent pedestrian, there beats beneath a layer of civilisation the twisted heart of an illegal meter-feeder and abuser of the double yellow line.

I don't know whether you've ever had stomach enough to watch traffic wardens on the prowl but if so, you may agree that they fall roughly into two categories. The first kind are brazen, prowling the streets with an indolent swagger, striking out suddenly to left or right, the kill swift, neat and terrible to observe, until sated with blood they knock off at about half-past six.

The other kind, usually smaller and older specimens, prefer to lurk in shop doorways and, from such concealment, wait until a victim comes to rest at the kerb, whereupon they shuffle out with amazing speed to do their dreadful work and then return, cackling, to their lair.

Now I shouldn't like to imply that I'm prejudiced against traffic wardens; since their only prey is the gaudy and frivolous motorist I regard them as a necessary part of nature's great design. To watch a motorist struggling in a traffic warden's grip is like watching a fly in a spider's web.

You may think it's cruel but if you're wise you don't interfere. You console yourself with the thought that this is merely nature at work and walk on, reflecting that as the spider survives by absorbing the blood of the fly, so the traffic warden derives his sustenance from the flibbertigibbet motorist.

Until recently all this seemed to be an unchanging fact of life. For the traffic warden to be other than he is was as improbable as the leopard turning up in the guise of a gentle pussy-cat. But then quite unexpectedly the traffic warden has started to mutate, as evidence of which I cite an advertisement that I came across in the Tube.

"Get out and about this summer," it said. "Be a traffic warden." There followed, beneath a picture of a traffic warden going about his business, some light talk of remuneration. But what struck me as significant (apart from the slogan) was the pictorial image of the warden himself.

He was not, as one might have supposed, an embittered, middle-aged, retired corporal with a tobacco-stained moustache, slapping tickets on car windscreens with demonic glee.

On the contrary, he was young and personable and though, as I recall, parked cars figured in the background he was actually ignoring them, his attention being devoted to a pair of dolly birds, foreign tourists at a guess and pedestrians both without a doubt.

He was smiling and they were ogling and all three had their heads bent over a book in which he was obviously taking down their telephone number with the object of arranging some wild *partie à trois* at their hotel as soon as he came off duty.

It was an eye-opener to me. Combined with that thrilling exhortation to "get out and about this summer", the picture showed the traffic warden in a new light – a swashbuckling adventurer of the city streets, friend and comforter of lonely foreign girls, a tourist attraction in his own right, a courteous but excitingly dangerous summertime swinger.

I look at these fellows differently now, with respect and envy. And I can't help wondering whether a similar campaign might be applied to other occupations in which recruitment is not perhaps all that it might be.

"Get into the warm this winter," for instance. "Be a gas-meter reader" – with a picture of someone like Paul Newman in a Gas Board cap crammed into a cupboard with a négligé-clad housewife closely resembling Sophia Loren.

September 3, 1973

007 cc

"M paused to fill his pipe and light it. 'There's not a moment to lose, 007,' he said quietly. 'Better get your skates on.'

"'Right, sir,' said Bond. A few minutes earlier the 1933 gunmetal-grey drophead roller skates (adaptable at the touch of a switch for instant ice-skating) with the Amherst-Villiers conversion and the flick knife concealed in each wheel had been brought round from the boot cupboard where he kept them. Within seconds Bond's powerful thrusting calf muscles were causing sparks to fly from the pavements of Whitehall as he set off in pursuit of his arch enemy. Somewhere up ahead, he knew, was Goldfinger on his supercharged pogo stick. Bond's eyes narrowed. Would he be in time . . ?"

As you can see I've been rewriting the James Bond books to bring them into line with the demands of the present fuel crisis, a modest act of patriotism for which I expect no reward. Propaganda of this kind is clearly going to be necessary in the months ahead and I have plenty of ideas to offer.

For instance, *Z Cars* will have to go for a start. Can't have the BBC wasting petrol by sending toy policemen up and down the streets of Newtown. The only problem is, will *Z Bikes* have quite the same appeal for a mass audience?

Mind you, in the old days, when the world was a well-ordered place, none of this would have been necessary. We'd simply have sent a gunboat and an expeditionary force.

We wouldn't, I can tell you, have sat back gritting our teeth while that Saudi Arabian chappy Sheikh Yamoney (accompanied, I shouldn't be at all surprised, by an even more militant adviser called Sheikh Yaphist) swaggered about Europe doing one-night stands on TV and threatening fearful consequences unless Golders Green were handed back to the Yemenis.

Indeed not. We'd have been straight up the Suez Canal, across to Cairo, kicking a few Wogs and Fuzzy-Wuzzies on the way, and instructing the cringing Sadat (the Egyptian leader, I mean, not his romantic cousin Sadat Yulbemein or the imploring Spanish nobleman Don Sadat) to stop behaving like a cad, grab himself a pick and shovel and start digging for oil before we really get cross.

Ted thought about it, naturally, but had to abandon the idea because his garage wouldn't let him have the petrol. After all, how far can a gunboat get on three gallons?

165

It was suggested at the Cabinet meeting the other day that Chay Blyth might be armed with a musket and sent across in his rowing boat to have a few stern words with someone or other but unfortunately he was a bit busy at the time. And Ted offered to go himself in *Morning Cloud* only he wasn't sure if he knew the way.

So there we are. The situation is grim and the only source of comfort we can find is in the Government's forthright statement that petrol rationing will not be introduced until after Christmas, unless of course it's introduced before Christmas.

Either way an age of austerity looms ahead for us all, or at least for all except those ingenious people who can convert their cars to run on methane gas manufactured from a handful of pig manure. A glimmer of hope there, I suppose, though I don't know. If the alternative is to go about picking up handfuls of pig manure I think I'd rather walk anyway.

Not that I mind the crisis a great deal for myself. I don't much like cars at the best of times because they invariably come apart in my hands. Besides, mine are always getting stolen or looted. If anyone has missed his last train and seeks alternative transport, or finds himself unexpectedly short of a car radio, or needs a few spare parts to get his own vehicle on the road, he automatically looks around to see where I've parked.

Still, that kind of worry is in the past. The age of the car is over. There'll be no Motor Show next year, you realised that, didn't you? It's another of my ideas. I'm having the Horse of the Year Show transferred to Earls Court where it will take on an entirely new meaning. There'll be half-naked model girls draped on every animal's withers, a six-month waiting list for two-tone thoroughbreds, Shetland ponies delivered immediately and shoes and blinkers available as optional extras.

However, back to 007 . . .

"As he skated into Hyde Park, Bond knew it was a losing battle. Goldfinger's pogo stick was too fast for him. There was only one thing for it – he'd have to get a rickshaw . . ."

November 26, 1973

Sylph Love Story

"There's a girl here," said Richard Burton, the other day in Milan, "who's madly in love with you."

"With me?" I said.

"Yes. She says you're so handsome, so lean, so English-looking."

"True," I said, for my natural honesty forbade me to deny it. "But, er who is she?"

"I'll tell you later," he said.

"Tell me now!" I said. "I'm leaving in a minute. Who is she?" It's not that I cared, you understand, good heavens, no. It just grieved me, that's all, to think that some poor girl was shyly eating her heart out for love of me and I was unable even to offer consolation by smiling sympathetically upon her and gently squeezing her hand.

Since I had no idea who she might be my position was rather delicate. I could hardly flit about the hotel smiling sympathetically upon and gently squeezing the hand of every girl I met. Some of them, hard though it may be to believe, might not be madly in love with me. They might even have nasty husbands who would take unkindly to their wives being smiled at and squeezed by a total stranger, no matter how handsome, lean and English-looking.

"Never mind that," said Mr Burton and then, of course, he changed the subject and started talking about himself. It's always the same with these actors.

They never want to discuss really important things; all they want to do is tell you about themselves. And he started telling me how much he loved his wife, so I was able to cross one name off the list anyway. Whoever it was who was madly in love with me it seemed reasonable to assume that it wasn't Elizabeth Taylor. Besides, she was in Rome at the time, as Mr Burton pointed out gloomily. They'd only recently been re-united after some trifling marital misunderstanding and now they'd been separated again for professional reasons, for thirty-six hours and he missed her sorely.

"Yes," I said, "Well, that's your problem. Listen, this girl . . ."

"I've been reading this book," he said. "Biography of Frieda Lawrence and old D. H. Terrible pair, those two, always quarrelling. Worse than Elizabeth and me, they were."

"Look here," I said, "we can talk about you any time. Just tell me, will you . . ."

"Acting," said Mr Burton, reflectively. "I don't understand it, you know. I don't understand people like Olivier and Gielgud and Elizabeth and Sophia Loren. Dedicated, they are. Couldn't live without acting. I could. I'm an actor by accident and sometimes I wish I wasn't one at all. I keep trying to retire but life costs so much I just have to keep going."

Well, I'd noticed he was still wearing last year's mink coat and that for the location filming of his latest movie, *The Voyage* (co-star Miss Loren; director Vittorio de Sica) he'd brought only the bare necessities of life – his manager, his chauffeur, his make-up man, his secretary – but I hadn't realised things were that tough.

So, putting aside personal matters for the moment, I murmured words of sympathy. He sighed. "I've got this bloody dog to support, you see," he said. He had the dog on his lap, a vicious one-eyed Pekingese called E'en So that had already taken at least a pound of flesh out of the publicity man. There are those who would say that this revealed it to be a dog of remarkable discernment but since it betrayed an equal desire to savage me I don't altogether go along with that.

"Richard," I said, "is it the girl I was chatting up in bed this morning?" (Actually, only she was in bed – for a scene in the film. Big, gorgeous Italian bird. I merely happened to be on the set, passing the time of day.)

He took no notice. "I'm feeling slightly apocalyptic," he said. "Elizabeth's daughter Liza, sixteen years old, said to me the other day, 'Daddy, where will I be in twenty years?' and I said, 'You'll have been divorced three times and the world will blow up.' "

"Yes," I said. "Quite. But, Richard, who is she?"

"Liza?" he said. "I told you – Elizabeth's daughter."

"No, no," I said, "not Liza. This other girl . . ."

But he'd gone. Back to the set. I don't think he ever intended to tell me really. Jealous, I expect, because she was madly in love with me and not with him. They're very conceited, you know, these actors.

January 14, 1974

Decide Issues

A group of researchers in America has just released the information that, by and large, and all things considered, the average man spends between two and four years of his allotted lifespan engaged in the business of simply making up his mind. Decisions, decisions. On the one hand . . . and yet, on the other hand . . .

Well, if it takes the average man that long there's an obvious cue here for anti-feminist jokes about how long it takes the average women to make up her mind but, fortunately, the researchers don't go into that. I expect they haven't made up their minds yet.

Nor, incidentally, do they tell us how long it took them to make up their minds to conduct a survey into how long it took people to make up their minds, although if they were smart – and anyone who can swing a job like that, which beats working generally and is certainly a great deal better than coal mining, must be awfully cute – they'd have spent the statutory two to four years on full salary and in a state of earnest indecision.

Quite likely they met every day in a comfortable office in some such building as the Rockefeller Center and tossed ideas back and forth until it was knocking off time. And every now and then someone from the foundation that was employing them would shout through the keyhole, "Hey, you guys, what's it to be? What are you going to research for us, fellers?"

And they'd all yell back in chorus, "We haven't made up our minds yet!" and roll about the carpet, slapping their thighs, while somebody sent out for another round of drinks. Actually, if the researchers were average men, running true to form, it's very possible that they've been engaged on this survey since it was first discovered that there was a pleasant living to be made out of asking people daft questions.

For instance, having made up their minds to conduct research into how long it took people to make up their minds, the next logical question for them to ask themselves would have been: "How do we go about it?" Well, there's another two to four years gone before, all other possibilities having been considered and rejected, somebody says, "Why don't we just ask people?"

But then, of course, as they're all sharpening their pencils and gathering up their notebooks ready to sally forth, someone else says, "Yeah, but hang on – who are we going to ask?" At which point the leader of the research group gets on the phone to the head of the foundation and says, "We're pretty nearly there, J. J. – just give us another two to four years . . ."

The process is endless. It's not even finished when they've made up their minds whom to approach and approached him. For, inevitably, as soon as they say, "Listen, Mac, we're, ah, engaged on a little research here. Would you mind telling us how long it takes you to make up your mind?" The subject, being an average man, says, "Well, gee, it's kinda hard to make up my mind about that. Do you wanna come back in two to four years' time?"

But still not everybody takes quite so long about it. When Michael O'Neill, a prisoner at Brixton gaol, was told the other day that he was to be released on bail it can hardly have taken him two to four seconds to make up his mind to get the hell out of there as quickly as possible; particularly as he must have known, none better, that they'd got the wrong Michael O'Neill and the right Michael O'Neill was still in his cell wondering why they were taking so long to make up their minds to let him out on bail. And even while that was going on the man who had made up his mind to stand surety had just changed his mind and was making up his mind not to.

All this tells us, however, is that the exception proves the rule and certainly I don't wish to suggest that this kind of research is useless. Handled properly it can be used to read the future. In the light of what we now know, it's clear that when the electorate returned a Labour government in 1966, it was actually engaged in making up its mind to vote Tory, which it did in 1970, at what time it was beginning to make up its mind to vote Labour, which – two to four years having elapsed – it will most surely do on February 28. Unless, of course, it votes Liberal. The trouble with the American survey is that while it tells us how long it takes the average man to make up his mind, it doesn't reveal what it is that he's made up his mind to do.

February 18, 1974

Tomb Stoned

It was a shrewd decision by the National Funeral Directors' Association of America to hold their convention in Las Vegas this year. At least it should convince them that there really is life of a sort after death.

Indeed, every funeral director who ever nursed a deep-rooted pessimism about the ultimate destination of his customers should certainly go there once, if only so that he can later stand beside a coffin consoling the bereaved and say with utter conviction, "Look on the bright side – wherever he's headed for, it can't be worse than Vegas." On neither side of the grave is there anything worse than Vegas.

It's not just the vulgarity of the place that makes the visitor swear to lead a better life in future if only someone will give him another chance and let him out, although to do it justice the vulgarity itself is kind of awe-inspiring. None of it could have been possible without demonic assistance, since no man born of woman – or anyway no man born without cloven hooves and a forked tail – could ever get to be that vulgar in a single lifetime.

Nor is it just the little, thoughtful touches that fill your soul with horror and despair – the one-armed bandits peering morbidly over your shoulder in the lavatory; the permanent midnight inside the buildings; the windows that never open; the bleak legions of the damned with their paper cups full of nickles, dimes and quarters to offer as sacrifices to the implacable machines; the total absence of clocks, so that after a while you don't know what hour it is or even what day, week, month, season or year it is. Time suspended, as in eternity.

Even if you've never been to Las Vegas you probably know about these things. You may also know that in the hotels the phones ring all the time and the public-address system keeps announcing calls for Arnold Schwartz, Herman T. Jones, and Mickey Rooney. Since none of these people are ever there I suspect the calls aren't genuine at all but are actually a system devised by the Mafia to announce that there are contracts out for them to be killed.

Possibly, too, you know that every bedroom has a peep-hole so that before opening the door you can decide whether the friendly neighbourhood mugger standing without is acceptable or not. But what you may not know is that you probably won't be able to identify whoever it was that pushed the bell anyway, because the chances are that he's lying dead on the floor before you can get the door open.

What nobody ever tells you about Las Vegas is that the static electricity is virtually lethal, due to a combination of dry climate and the hoteliers' habit of carpeting everywhere with deep-pile accept-no-imitation, Wilton-type Nylon. No matter what you touch you end up bouncing off the opposite wall. Adjust the volume control on the telly and lightning streaks across the room. Even getting out of your room is dangerous unless you've mastered the art of hurling your key into the keyhole like a dart. I daresay people have gone mad or starved to death or both while trying to learn the trick.

So, as you stumble to bed after another disastrous session of blackjack in the small hours of the morning – or what you assume to be the small hours of the morning, although it might just as easily be lunchtime – the air is full of the smell of burning flesh and the pitiful moans of people trapped in their rooms, being slowly fried to death by small charges of electricity.

Actually, very few people go to bed in Las Vegas and I think I know why. For a start, the bed itself is probably big enough to stage a seven-a-side rugby match and is round and white with a sunken bath beside it. And if you're really unlucky it could have a mirrored ceiling above it too.

Imagine, if you can, the horror of waking from troubled sleep to see yourself staring down from the ceiling with the charred fingertips and scarlet, haunted eyes of one who, having clearly been plucked from life betimes and deserving nothing worse than Purgatory, finds himself unfairly banished to Las Vegas.

A bad scene, no doubt. But unless you've been there you can't begin to understand the desolation that assails you when you remember that you're not even dead yet but you're in Las Vegas anyway.

March 25, 1974

Trusty Prints

I admired, as I'm sure we all did, the picture of Mrs Williams being transmuted into the trusty and well-beloved Marcia Matilda Falkender, Baroness Falkender of West Haddon in Northampton-shire.

Very cute she was in her ducky little cap and robe, a touch of ermine at the throat and what looked like a bow-tie nestling under her right ear and apparently making its way round to the back of her neck.

But what I'd like to know is: what happened to the other picture? Aha, you ask, what other picture is that? Well, let me set the scene.

Just before the trusty and well-beloved Baroness took her seat in the Lords, the press photographers were waiting outside her house to capture the historic moment when she sallied forth and a law student approached one of them to ask whether he was thirsty.

Yes, said the photographer, he was, as a matter of fact – very thirsty. Whereupon, inspired either by a misplaced sense of gallantry or – this being the vacation and he having had no opportunity to take part in or even witness a college riot for some weeks – by withdrawal symptoms, the student (showing a subtlety of wit that augurs well for his future in the Temple) emptied a bucket of water over him.

The photographer, however, being clearly a man with no discernible sense of humour, waxed exceeding wrath and, pursuing the student, began to clobber him.

At this point the door of the house opened and who should emerge, wearing dressing-gown and curlers, but the trusty and well-beloved Marcia Matilda Falkender, Baroness Falkender of West Haddon in Northamptonshire, demanding to know – though no doubt employing a more elegant turn of phrase as befits anyone so trusty and well-beloved – what the cuffing heck was going on.

And that's the picture I'm talking about – the picture of the trusty and well-beloved Baroness in her equally trusty and well-beloved dressing-gown and curlers. I've not seen it published anywhere so I can only assume that (a) press photographers are not what they were and (b) that my friend Monty was not among those present.

My friend Monty is a prince among photographers and once, as a boy gossip writer, I was privileged to be with him in Switzerland on the occasion of Princess Alexandra's very first skiing holiday.

There were about six of us, reporters and photographers, following her about and Monty was our spokesman. "Hello darlin'," he said, greeting the Princess on the nursery slopes. (I don't really think there was a sufficient degree of intimacy between them to justify such a salute but Monty was not the man to hold that against her. He simply wanted her to feel among friends.) "Just takin' a few snaps, darlin'. You don't mind, do you?"

Whether she minded or not she merely smiled wanly and set about learning to ski, with us trudging faithfully up and down Alps in her wake.

And a strange sight we must have looked, some of us, in our trendy London gear. It was the age, I think, of the Chelsea boot and I'm here to say that if you happened to tread on an icy Alp in a leather-soled Chelsea boot you didn't actually need a ski to reach the bottom in record time.

Anyway, Monty and his colleagues took pictures all day until at last the Princess buttonholed him and said, "Look, you've got hundreds of photographs. Surely you're happy now?"

And Monty said: "Oh, I'm happy darlin', but is my editor going to be happy? I mean, I'll send these snaps back to London and my editor will look through 'em and he'll say 'All very well' he'll say 'but where's the one of her fallin' flat on her arse?' I can't leave here darlin' till I've got a picture of you fallin' flat on your arse."

The Princess sighed, "Oh, very well," she said and, skiing slowly down the slope, collapsed gracefully into the snow opposite Monty's camera.

"Just hold it there," said Monty. "Big smile. One more. Lovely, lovely. Ta, darlin', you're a princess."

So I can't help feeling, you see, that had Monty been around during the fracas outside Baroness Falkender's home he would not only have photographed the lady in dressing-gown and curlers but he would also have contrived to photograph her slipping in the water from the law student's bucket and landing neatly on her trusty and well-beloved . . . well, you know. And what's more with a big smile, too.

July 29, 1974

Bowler Rice

The Japanese Government, it says here, is spending £12 millions on a special institute for the grooming of local business executives into typical English gentlemen of the public-school variety.

In what is described as "an intensive one-year course" they're taught how to hold a fork and make small talk, what to say if the food is inedible (you wave aside your hostess's charred Yorkshire pudding with a polite smile and, after consulting page 8 of the good form manual, murmur, "No thank you. Doctor's orders . . .") and how to treat a lady. How you treat a lady is you offer her your arm, help her off with her coat and fill her glass at a party.

At the end of this intensive course the Japanese executive has been transformed into an Oriental facsimile of a graduate of Eton and Balliol able, with the aid of his handbook, to slip easily into society and the Old Boy network.

All very commendable and rather flattering. But what bothers me is the thought that if trade between Nippon and Britain is such that Japanese businessmen are being groomed in our ways there's a fair chance that our businessmen are also being groomed in theirs. And this could lead to possible confusion when the two cultures meet . . .

Scene I: The office of an English businessman of public-school education. The internal phone rings. Secretary: "Mr Tojo is here, sir."

"Who?"

"Mr Tojo, sir. Of the Imperial Nipponese Cricket Box and Athletic Support Company."

"Oh, my God!" English businessman feverishly consults manual on Japanese behaviour. Page 2, rule 7, sub-section IVA: "Always remove shoes indoors."

English businessman kicks Hush Puppies into corner as door opens and Japanese businessman enters, removing gloves and bowler. Englishman rises, bowing and making hissing noises.

"What ho, what ho. Frightful weather, what?"

"Ah so, Tojo-san. Please to take seat."

Japanese sits, balancing bowler on one knee and sucking knob of cane with vacuous English-public-school expression. Englishman composes face into inscrutable smile and tucks hands into sleeves of Burton's Younger Executive worsted-type suit. "Tojo-san, you rike runch?"

"Runch?" Japanese executive furtively produces handbook and thumbs through glossary of well-known English-public-school phrases seeking "runch". "Sorry, old boy. Rather fear you've caught me out with that one."

Englishman's inscrutable smile fades slightly at realisation that stupid little Nip can't even understand own language. "You rike eat?" Makes motions of bearing chopsticks to mouth.

"Eat? Ah, you mean lunch."

Englishman furtively produces handbook and thumbs through glossary of well-known Japanese phrases seeking "lunch". "Eat, eat. Loast beef. Ramb chops. Sukiyaki!"

Japanese nods making signs of handling knife and fork and taking mental note that English word "runch" means some kind of food.

"Ah, so Tojo-san."

"Oh, quite, old boy." Exeunt.

Scene II: The same, three hours later. Enter Englishman alone, limping badly and wearing tattered socks having forgotten to put on Hush Puppies when leaving for lunch. He sinks into chair, demanding large whisky from secretary.

"My God, what a day! Took the little swine to the Savoy. Couldn't talk to him, of course – didn't seem to understand a blind word I said. Appears to be obsessed by the bloody weather. I tried to make him feel at home – I sat on the floor, bowing and hissing and eating Vichyssoise with chopsticks. (Can't think why, but he tried it with a fork.) Anyway, old Cholmondeley and his good lady joined us. Relief at hand, I thought but the bloody little Nip went mad. Raving sex maniac! Grabbed Mrs Cholmondeley by the arm and started ripping her clothes off. No, I promise you! Fortunately, I stopped him before he got past her coat but then he fell to plying her with liquor. Every time she took a sip he filled her glass. Pissed as a newt she was before we'd finished the avocado. Can't imagine

175

what he saw in her – she's fifty-five if she's a day. Old Cholmondeley took it like a gentleman, of course, until we left and the Nip grabbed her arm again and then he really had to intercede. I couldn't stand it, I'm afraid. Left the three of them fighting in the foyer . . ."

Another thought occurs to me. What if this Japanese innovation spreads throughout the Far East? "I say, I say, I say. Who was that Oriental gentleman I saw you with last night?"

"That was no Oriental gentleman. That was my old school Thai."

December 2, 1974

Nurse a Thick Year

Even the most optimistic among us could hardly claim, as we stand here among the still smouldering wreckage of 1974, that the new year had got off to a particularly felicitous start.

As the last roof beam of the old year collapsed, the words "Burmah Oil" being just discernible on its charred surface, it occurred to me that the best thing would be to cancel 1975 entirely and move straight into 1976. There's much to be said for this, actually, when you consider the tasks that confront us in the forthcoming twelve months.

For a start we have to get rid of all those Trotskyite teachers who, according to Dr Rhodes Boyson, have infiltrated the education system, and are even now turning our primary schools into miniature Red Armies. You can easily tell the Trotskyite teachers because they wear crumpled jeans and quite probably have long hair and beards as well.

Some pretend they look like that because they're not very well-paid and can afford neither decent clothes nor haircuts and razor blades, but Dr Boyson knows better, and eternal vigilance is demanded if we are not to discover one morning that the Government has been taken over by heavily armed eight-year-olds with snow on their boots.

But an even more insidious menace confronts us. At a Get Britain Out of Europe conference in London, Mr Richard Body, Tory M.P. for Holland and Boston, revealed that the crafty French have so manipulated the Common Market that our very eating habits are about to be changed. Under the new import levies, said Mr Body, traditional British delicacies such as tomato soup and prawn cocktail could vanish from our menus, to be replaced by (ugh!) frogs' legs and (yuk!) snails.

So, as we force down frogs' legs and snails under the stern gaze of tiny Red soldiers, how are we to cope with the demands of European Architectural Heritage Year, to say nothing of International

Woman's Year? I was going to suggest that, to save time, money and effort, they could be combined into one event – a sort of International Women's Architectural Heritage Year, a more rewarding field of study for men at any rate. But when I remembered how violently even the mildest women react these days if you suggest they might be attractive and desirable, without also adding that each of them has the brain of Einstein and a faster left jab than Muhammad Ali, I thought better of it.

Where then is hope to be sought as 1975 already begins to creak upon its foundations and cracks appear in the plaster? Well, I found a glister of it in the report that a Middle Eastern oil sheikh was to bid for the Aston Martin company. True, this is probably just a piece of individual enterprise. No doubt the fellow runs a few Aston Martins and, having trouble getting them serviced out there in the desert, feels that he'd at least be in with a fighting chance of having his cars looked after if he bought the entire company.

But the principle is well worth supporting. Since the Arabs have all the money there is anyway, why don't we just sell them the whole country? Of course, it would mean changes in our lifestyle. I daresay we'd have to hand over the throne to, say, the Shah of Persia, while the leaders of our own political parties could hardly aspire to any loftier role than that of joint Chief Eunuch.

The indigenous population might have to accustom itself to somewhat humbler careers, such as shining shoes, selling feelthy postcards and offering its sister to any passer-by.

But we'd soon adapt ourselves to the idea of buying our undies from Arafat and Yamani (formerly trading under the name of Marks and Spencer), and if the Arabs diplomatically arranged the marriage of Prince Charles to the daughters of four oil sheikhs in a ceremony at Westminster Mosque conducted by the Archmoslem of Canterbury, I imagine we'd be easy-going enough to accept the altered circumstances.

The main thing, after all, is that Britain would be rich. Even the French and the Trotskyites wouldn't be daft enough to try to screw the Arabs, and we'd be able to eat our tomato soup and prawn cocktails in peace.

January 6, 1975

True Brit

The tourist season starts again next month, and if they've all been studying their guidebooks carefully I can see it's going to be even more fun than usual.

After a few hours spent conning his guidebooks, the happy foreign tourist will arrive on these shores with a pretty fair idea of

178

what to expect. For instance, according to one book, he'll find that the British are "a handsome, sturdy people – clean-limbed, clear-skinned, with the muscular co-ordination of athletes"; while according to another, the Englishman has "a childlike quality to his spirit – a charming, puckish, stubborn refusal to grow up. When you dig under his skin you'll find passion, gaiety, richness, all the human values of your next door neighbour".

Glossing over these extraordinary claims for a moment, let us move on to the question of vocabulary. "Homely", says one book, means hard-working, "khaki" is patois for horse-manure and, by extension presumably, any other kind of manure and, as every Cockney knows, "barley fair" is rhyming slang for hair. Got that, you foreigners? Right, well now we come to the important bit: "If it's your habit to ask for the john, you'll get a polite and vacant stare; but if you ask for the 'claude' you'll find a sympathetic soul."

Okay, let's test it out. Assume that you're a foreign tourist caught in Oxford Street and extremis. You rush up to the nearest passer-by with desperate urgency and say: "Pliss can you me to der claude direct? I vish her khaki to make."

Now if you're lucky and you've chosen a handsome, sturdy person – clean-limbed, clear-skinned and with the muscular coordination of an athlete – you've very probably hit upon another foreign tourist who's read the same guidebook as you and, being therefore able to understand the language, will turn out to be a sympathetic soul.

What is much more likely, however, is that you will have approached a squat, scowling, spotty person who has recently been made redundant and is shambling off to draw the dole, and who will suggest crisply that you cuff off back where you came from, and who will go on his way muttering that old Enoch was quite right and he didn't know what the country was coming to, blowed if he did, when an Englishman couldn't walk the streets of London without being accosted by filthy foreign poofters calling him Claude.

An even nastier fate awaits the tourist who holds the popular belief that English girls are the easiest game in the world, and goes in search of good-natured company. Whether he attempts to ingratiate himself with a languid salesgirl by saying: "*Mein* vord, vot a homely girl you are" or approaches some well-stacked strawberry blonde vision with a suggestive wink and the words: "Excuse pliss, I am your fine barleys admiring . . ." he'll almost certainly find himself reeling from the scene of the encounter bleeding heavily from the nose and wondering whatever happened to that charming puckish quality of the English, that passion, gaiety and richness and all those human values of one's next door neighbour.

The fact is, of course, that the average Briton is not handsome and sturdy, clean-limbed and clear-skinned with the muscular coordination of an athlete. I am – but the average Briton is not.

Nor would he take kindly to being described as "charmingly puckish, passionate and gay" – especially gay – while his human values as a next-door-neighbour extend no further than hammering violently on the party-wall with instructions to turn that cuffing record player down, there are people here trying to watch telly.

The average Briton is usually slightly cross and discontented with his lot and suffers from muscular twinges through living in all that damp. He hates foreign tourists bitterly because they're richer than he is and also because they either speak his language better than he does or else communicate in a kind of guidebook English comprehensibly only to other students of guidebook English.

Furthermore, he is sick of disparaging guidebook references to his meals which consist of "industrially-made soup and a plate of meat, always boiled or braised, accompanied by a choice of vegetables tasting of water". That happens to be exactly how the average Briton likes his food, and if foreign tourists don't fancy it, well, he didn't ask them to come here, did he?

And if his country is going to be invaded any minute now by lunatic foreigners trying to grope English girls' barleys and expecting the indigenous population to answer to the name of Claude, they'd better not be surprised when the khaki hits the fan.

March 3, 1975